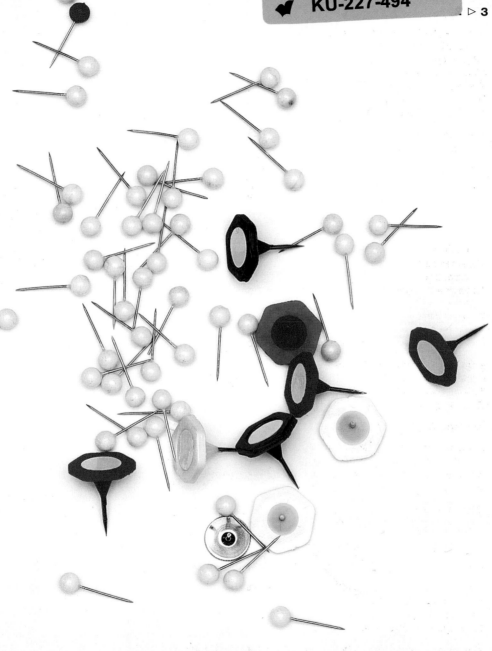

Table of contents

4

5

6

This book provides a broad and detailed look at art direction as a process that is used to communicate an advertising message in a manner that is attention-grabbing, visually compelling and consistent with the creative and strategic objectives of a brand. It also examines the role of the art director and the creative team in general, from the initial stages of idea generation through to the final stages of production.

Within the following chapters, you'll find useful tips and words of advice on how to hone your art-direction skills, improve your creative portfolio (or book), and ultimately, land your first job as an advertising creative. Examples of great advertising campaigns from across the world are used to illustrate the key themes of each chapter and practical exercises are included within the text, providing you with an opportunity to try some of this out for yourself.

Chapter navigation
Clear navigation is provided to help you find your way around the book.

Headings
Prominent section headings enable you to quickly locate a topic of interest.

Captions
Revealing explanations illustrate how adverts achieve their impact.

A way with words
Useful definitions of key words and advertising phrases are supplied.

Give it a go
Practical exercises are provided to enable you to test and enhance the skills you will learn over the course of using this book.

Summaries
Succinct, thought-provoking commentaries are supplied on the main text.

Direct

Direct advertising is distinguished from other forms of advertising by the manner in which it sets out to communicate and engage more directly with the target audience, through a variety of different media such as direct mail, telemarketing, email and a range of online formats. Although recipients are targeted through the use of sophisticated databases, direct advertising material is usually unsolicited; therefore, if it's not well considered and designed, it runs the risk of being ignored, or worse still, annoying the recipient – as in the case of junk mail. More distinctively, direct advertising will incorporate a 'call to action' that requires a direct response from the recipient.

Art directing direct advertising

Direct advertising material is normally just one component of a much bigger integrated campaign. It's therefore important for the art director to have a broad view of how the direct advertising will integrate with the rest of the campaign, both in terms of concept and appearance. Art direction itself will typically be focused on graphic media such as online material, press ads and direct mail.

As direct advertising is often concerned with developing a lasting relationship with the recipients, there should be a sense of continuity flowing through the design and layout of these adverts. Both the art direction and the overall design of the advert should have a sense of 'one-to-one' communication embedded within them. You'll need to work closely with your copywriter to achieve this.

Right
**'Rescue the vegetables' –
Promoting a direct response!**
This integrated direct response campaign identified the fact that every single day in the UK, food is thrown away and wasted. The call to action – 'Your country veg needs YOU!' – urged the audience to rescue unwanted vegetables by adding Knorr Stock cubes to the cooking ingredients. The campaign humorously mimicked the format of political campaign posters and followed the traditional pre-Christmas media scheduling normally used by charity campaigns.
Agency: JWT London
Client: Unilever

A way with words: Call to action

Literally interpreted, the term 'call to action' is a statement that summons the consumer to act. It normally urges immediate action and in its most basic form uses common terms such as 'call now', 'write now' or 'click here'. It refers to the means by which you motivate your audience to take the next step and respond to your advert. Above all, the call to action has to be compelling enough to elicit the desired response. In other words, you have to give the recipient a good reason to respond. This reason could be something as simple as a limited offer, a special discount, or any other incentive that moves them emotionally to take instant action.

Integrated media campaigns

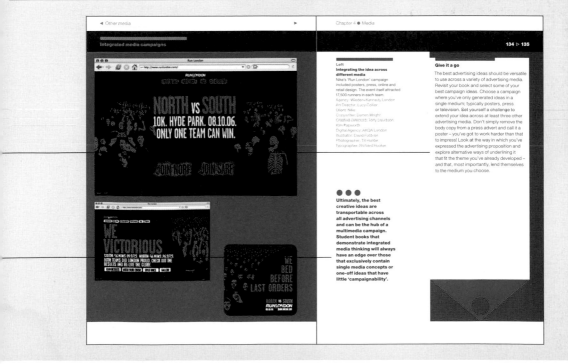

Left
**Integrating the idea across
different media**
Nike's 'Run London' campaign included posters, press, online and retail design. The event itself attracted 17,500 runners in each team.
Agency: Wieden+Kennedy London
Art Director: Lucy Collier
Client: Nike
Copywriter: Darren Wright
Creative Directors: Tony Davidson, Kim Papworth
Digital Agency: AKQA London
Illustrator: David Foldvari
Photographer: Til Hunter
Typographer: Richard Hooke

● ● ●
Ultimately, the best creative ideas are transportable across all advertising channels and can be the hub of a multimedia campaign. Student books that demonstrate integrated media thinking will always have an edge over those that exclusively contain single media concepts or one-off ideas that have little 'campaignability'.

Give it a go

The best advertising ideas should be versatile to use across a variety of advertising media. Revisit your book and select some of your best campaign ideas. Choose a campaign where you've only generated ideas in a single medium; typically posters, press or television. Set yourself a challenge to extend your idea across at least three other advertising media. Don't simply remove the body copy from a press advert and call it a poster – you've got to work harder than that to impress! Look at the way in which you've expressed the advertising proposition and explore alternative ways of underlining it that fit the theme you've already developed – and that, most importantly, lend themselves to the medium you choose.

Any advertising creative will tell you that the most important element of an advert is the idea itself, and if you get this right, the rest will follow. However, once the 'big idea' has surfaced, the process of crafting that idea in a manner that expresses it in the most powerful and memorable visual fashion becomes the next task for the art director to focus on.

The best art direction grabs attention to the advertising message without grabbing attention to itself. It should engage the audience and draw them into the concept without getting in the way of communication. Art direction has to be the transport for the idea, which naturally has to come first.

As with most aspects of creativity, the craft of art directing advertising ideas is one that tends to defy any attempt to be pinned down to an exact science and what's more, it's full of paradoxes. Having said that, there is such a thing as good art direction and, of course, poor art direction. What this book sets out to do is to provide you with some advice, guidelines and principles that will keep you on the right track and, hopefully, make sure that you're producing more of the 'good stuff'.

The book is divided into six key themes:

Chapter 1
The role of the art director

An overview of art direction as a process. What exactly it is and how it works as a tool for communicating the advertising message. The multi-faceted role of the art director as one half of the 'creative team' is examined in this chapter. How the art director and copywriter work together during the initial briefing stage to brainstorm ideas and explore different routes and creative strategies is reviewed. The various other tasks that are involved, from visualising the concept and working with illustrators, photographers, typographers and commercial directors, through to post production and the final stages of seeing the job through, are also explored.

Chapter 2
The tools of art direction

The ability to see things differently and art direct an image in a fashion that enables your audience to see things differently as well, is at the heart of good art direction. It's all about making the usual *unusual*, the familiar *unfamiliar*, and the ordinary *extraordinary*. The use of surprise, ambiguity, simplicity, understatement, drama, provocation, tension and eye-catching images are just a few of the tools you can use to get your message across.

Chapter 3
Creating the adverts

Understanding the brand, the needs and desires of the target audience and, of course, the advertising objectives is an essential part of the preparation that will lead to the 'big idea'. Once the creative team have an idea or a campaign concept established, the art director will explore a variety of visual layouts and alternative executions. The use of illustration, photography and typography have to be considered, alongside the use of live action, animation, computer-generated images and an array of post-production techniques that can be used to great effect. Visualising the ideas as rough 'scamps', or storyboards, is an essential stage in communicating the idea to the other parties involved in the production process.

Chapter 4
Media

Advertising media is the canvas upon which the 'big' creative idea is expressed. The choice of media can offer extra creative opportunities and it can sometimes be an integral part of the idea itself. Traditional forms of visual media such as posters, magazines, press, television and cinema, are today augmented with a wide array of new media and ambient media options. The manner in which different media integrate across the advertising campaign is an important consideration for the creative team and requires a sound understanding of the relationship between the various media and the audience for the advertising message.

Chapter 5
Ideas and inspiration

The creative brief is the starting point for all advertising creativity. It can inspire lateral thinking, idea exploration and even provide a few suggestions and insights that can kick-start the creative team in the right direction. However, the search for an idea can often be more about perspiration than inspiration (to paraphrase the inventor, Thomas Edison), and you can never pre-empt when or where the idea will surface. There are many different places we can search for the elusive idea and things we can do to help that idea surface sooner, rather than later. Key to this is an understanding of the principles of idea generation and the ability to tell when you have a good idea.

Chapter 6
Getting a job as an art director

The task of getting your first job as an art director begins with good planning and preparation. Creative talent is of course essential, but this alone may not be enough to ensure that you're doing all the right things; talking to the right people, getting the right advice and being in the right place at the right time. Getting your book (portfolio) organised is the first step, and knowing both what to include, and what to leave out, is an essential step towards achieving that important agency placement. Knowing what support and resources are available to help you find your first job is also important and can give you the edge in a competitive market.

The term 'art direction' is generally used to describe the process of organising and quite literally directing the visual elements of any communication media, be it a film, a television programme, a digital installation, a commercial or a print-based advert. In this sense, art direction is an activity that has a much broader application across a range of disciplines associated with visual communication.

For the purpose of this book, we'll be looking more specifically at the role of art direction within the field of advertising and the manner in which the skills of the art director are employed to achieve defined advertising goals and objectives.

What art direction is (and what it isn't)

In very basic terms, art direction involves designing the 'look' of the advert. However, this task involves more than just aesthetic considerations. It's not just about making the advert look nice. In the end, the visual elements comprising the advert have to work together in a way that maximises the impact of the advertising message itself. This can often mean that some of the more traditional principles of graphic design or aesthetic conventions are abandoned in order to achieve the communication objectives.

Agency: AMV BBDO
Client: The Economist
Creatives: Matthew Abbott,
Martin Casson

Above
**Breaking the rules or
redefining them?**
Who said that print adverts need
headlines or even logos? Breaking
conventions is one way to wake up
your audience and grab their attention.
The bold use of colour and vacant
space adds to the effect in this poster
for The Economist, which implies
that the magazine is the missing part
of the puzzle.

What art direction is (and what it isn't)

When to break the rules (or not)

At this point, it's important to stress that it's not a case of just throwing out all the rules of design and allowing visual anarchy to rule the day. On the contrary, it's more a case of knowing when to break those rules and conventions in order to grab attention and create surprise, intrigue and tension or elicit any other emotional response from your audience that may help achieve the objectives set out in the creative brief. Of course, in order to break the rules and make that creative leap, you first need to have an understanding of what the rules are, and for advertising students this presents the first of many paradoxes: 'the first rule of advertising is that there aren't any rules!' The best way to come to terms with this concept is to re-interpret it as: 'in creative advertising, all rules can be challenged.' The same concept really applies to all creative design disciplines to varying degrees. If this weren't the case, advertising design, graphic design, product design and most other fields of design would result in products and artefacts that fail to offer anything fresh or original to the audiences and end-users for whom they were designed.

Once you're aware of the 'rules' and conventions associated with visual communication and design layout, you can start challenging them in order to keep your art direction looking fresh and original.

Art direction should help [an] idea rather than hinder it. Art direction should be a window rather than a beautifully painted and papered wall. Art direction should be simple and logical. It should be about the product and for the market it is aimed at. If people only get as far as admiring your ad for the look of it, then you've failed. Art direction can only be the transport, it can't be the whole journey.
David Christensen
Art Director
1996

But is it art?

The term 'art direction' can itself be misleading, depending on whether or not you view advertising as art. This question has been the topic of many undergraduate dissertations, and has fuelled substantial debate. It's also an issue that splits advertising practitioners, between those who do, and those who don't consider it to be art. There's a risk that in setting out to create a work of art, you can lose sight of those objectives – or put simply, the 'art' can get in the way of the advertising message.

Although it can be argued that advertising itself may not be art, it often borrows images from art or emulates distinctive artistic schools or styles in its visual execution. It does this for one purpose only – to communicate the message in the most effective and appropriate manner possible. So, in short, it's not just about art – it's about communication!

If you set out to create a piece of art, chances are that you'll end up compromising the advertising objectives. Remember: communication of the message has to come first.

The idea comes first

As a conduit for communication, art direction is the means by which the creative idea is visually expressed. It can never be a substitute for the idea itself. As another art director, Steve Dunn, once put it: 'The ad is the cake. The art direction is the icing.' He points out that if the advert isn't great, it's not worth art directing. Indeed, it's often the case that a great idea is still a great idea even if the art direction is poor. However, the best art direction in the world won't make a poor idea any better. With this in mind, it is important that the visual execution, styling, use of post-production effects or computer-generated images aren't seen as the 'big idea'. These methods and techniques may be part of the idea itself but it's very rarely the case that the central idea or concept is based solely on the visual execution.

What art direction is (and what it isn't)

◀ ▶

**Below and right
Advertising that borrows from art**
In this print campaign for
Harvey Nichols, surrealist art provides
a means of conveying themes such
as beauty, power, and attraction
in an unconventional manner for
a fashion store. The heavy use of
symbolism associated with this art
genre grabs attention and promotes
audience engagement.
Agency: DDB London
Art Director: Emer Stamp
Client: Harvey Nichols
Photographer: Dimitri Daniloff

HARVEY NICHOLS
WOMENSWEAR

KNIGHTSBRIDGE · DUBLIN · MANCHESTER · EDINBURGH · BIRMINGHAM · LEEDS

HARVEY NICHOLS
MENSWEAR

HARVEY NICHOLS
BEAUTY

What art direction is (and what it isn't)

Left

A strong central idea is the key to success

It may provide dramatic imagery that everyone remembers, but at the heart of this commercial lies a central campaign thought: that 'good things are worth waiting for'. This concept was based on the fact that it takes a full two minutes (or 119.5 seconds if you believe the marketing department) to pour the perfect pint of Guinness beer. Having a central idea like this enables you to generate further ideas and create a campaign based on a common theme. So remember, the idea must come first. Only then should you start to think about how best to present that idea in terms of visual layout, style and direction.

Agency: AMV BBDO
Client: Guinness

It could be the case that the visual execution may be the most memorable and attention-grabbing aspect of your advert, but there must still be a 'big idea' at the hub of it.

Formulating your central idea

A good example of the importance of having a central idea is the highly acclaimed commercial for the Guinness brand, created in 1999 by Abbott Mead Vickers BBDO. The advert features a group of surfers going out to sea and riding the waves, with white horses rising out of the wave crests and galloping above the surfer's heads. In 2000, the commercial was popularly voted the greatest TV advert of all time, in a poll run jointly by the UK's *The Sunday Times* and Channel 4. Amongst the accolades that this commercial received was a Gold Lion in Cannes (1999) and two Gold Design and Art Direction Awards in 2000.

At the time that this commercial was aired and for some years afterwards, audiences would often cite it as their favourite ad and it quickly acquired iconic status in the world of advertising. The dramatic black and white imagery (consistent with the brand theme and acting as a visual prompt of the two-tone appearance of a pint of Guinness beer) – combined with evocative camera direction, scripting, voiceover and music – all added to the impact and familiarity of this commercial. This example may seem to contradict the premise just mentioned that good art direction isn't there to be admired, but always remember that creative advertising is full of paradoxes! Ultimately, it was a central idea that came first: the concept that *good things are worth waiting for*.

How art direction works

Having taken a look at what exactly art direction is, it's worth briefly examining how art direction works, before tackling this in more detail in the chapters that follow. A good place to start is by looking at David Christensen's analogy of art direction as a 'window'. Just as a window is essentially a transparent medium that enables us to view things on the other side of it, good art direction enables us to see or understand the advertising message more clearly. It's all about clarity, and nothing that the art director adds should hinder, obstruct, or get in the way of that message. In this sense, the window in question is of course a clear pane, not a stained-glass affair. It's often tempting to start showing-off with clever graphic tricks and design wizardry, but it's essential to resist the temptation and always remember that 'less is more'... a theme that we'll be returning to in detail later in this book.

Art direction as a presentation

One way to understand the *mechanics* of art direction is to use another analogy; that of a personal presentation or pitch, whereby you the presenter are trying to sell an idea or concept to another person or a group of people. This needn't be an advertising pitch. It could just as easily be an idea for a new invention, or a business venture that you're trying to get someone to buy or invest in. As a presenter, you have an opportunity to use the face-to-face encounter to show and demonstrate what you have to offer. In such cases, the success or failure of your pitch is often determined not just by the quality of your idea, but also by the way in which you present it; including aspects such as your pace of delivery, the order and sequence of information, body language, confidence, attitude and sometimes the quality of your dramatic performance.

Now let's make the comparison with art direction. Having a great advertising idea for selling a product is essential, but first you have to grab your audience's attention, and generate their interest or desire in your product. Art direction plays a major role, using drama, intrigue, suspense, tension, surprise or revelation to achieve the desired effect and help sell the idea. In essence, the manner in which you art direct your advert *is* the visual presentation of the advertising message.

Don't forget it's a diesel.

Above
Simplicity aids clarity
A simple visual idea that
communicates in a clear, witty and
memorable fashion. Clever symbolism
is stripped of any other superfluous
visual elements that may get in the
way of the message – 'Don't forget
it's a diesel'.
Agency: DDB London
Client: Volkswagen
Creative Director: Jeremy Crisgan
Photographer: Jason Tozer

Below
**Mashed potato, or clouds in
the sky?**
In this advert for Lurpak butter, clever
art direction presents an image of
mashed potato, alluding to white
fluffy clouds in a blue sky, establishing
a link with the headline: 'Mash –
Food of the Gods'.
Agency: Wieden & Kennedy
Client: Lurpak
Creatives: Ben Walker, Matt Gooden

How art direction works

Concept cars. Aren't they fantastic?

Cars that park themselves. Cars that hover.

But are they only exciting because they never get made?

What if one actually made it onto the production line?

Like the Honda FCX. A car that runs on hydrogen.

Whose only emission is pure water.

Maybe then we'd call them 'reality cars'.

Do you believe in the power of dreams?

Creating a 'look' for the brand

A presenter will not only decide how to present information; he or she will also control the flow of information, in terms of what to present to the audience and at what stage to present it. Similarly, good art direction can also determine the manner in which the viewer interprets the message. By establishing a hierarchy of visual elements, the art director can control the sequence in which the viewer decodes the visual cues and various other aspects of the design layout to ascertain meaning.

To extend the analogy further, think about the kind of things that make a good presentation memorable. Nine times out of ten, it's likely to be something that's very different from every other presentation that your audience has seen; something quirky, unexpected or just unusual perhaps. The same applies to art direction.

The last thing you want your client's mobile phone advert to look like is every other mobile phone advert. Art direction can help create a distinct 'look' for your client that becomes synonymous with the brand personality.

The relationship between image and copy

Simply grabbing attention isn't enough; and the art direction of an advert has to work harder to get the reader to read on. The use of white space, the juxtaposition of image and copy and the use of ambiguity and intrigue are all aspects of advertising design that can compel the reader to start reading the body copy.

Good art direction works hand-in-hand with good copywriting. In most print-based adverts where there is both headline copy and an Image, each element should seek to complement the other. A headline shouldn't describe what the reader can already see in the image. Instead, it should complete the picture by adding meaning to it, or should aim to reframe the meaning originally interpreted from the image to provide a twist or unexpected outcome. Art direction determines the relationship between headline and image and can heighten the effect of the communication.

Left
Using space to grab attention
In this advert for the Honda FCX hydrogen-fuelled car, the bold and cryptic image, the generous use of white space and the conspicuous absence of a headline collectively draw the reader into the body copy, which explains that the only emission from this car is 'pure water'.
Agency: Wieden + Kennedy
Client: Honda

One of the most fundamental tasks of an art director is to make sure that image and copy work with each other, rather than compete against each other.

The creative team

It's important to remember that in most advertising agencies, the art director is only one half of the creative partnership – the copywriter being the other half. Together, the art director and copywriter are more commonly referred to as the creative team, and within the agency's creative department there can be any number of these teams (depending on the size of the agency) working under the supervision of a creative director.

There's no 'i' in team

Generally speaking, the art director and copywriter are jointly responsible for coming up with the creative ideas and central campaign concept together. Neither of them has the sole remit to have ideas. It's a team activity and even though either of them may initiate the concept and contribute more ideas to the process, both recognise that the winning idea for the next creative brief could just as easily come from the other partner.

First thoughts and first ideas

After the initial briefing, the art director and copywriter will spend considerable time together talking over the brief and discussing their options. At the same time, they may need to share a few initial thoughts about what they should and shouldn't be doing, in order to reach a common understanding of what they will be attempting to achieve with their ideas. Once the team feel that they have a clear understanding of the brand, the advertising objectives, the target audience and what they want to say to that audience, the tops can come off the marker pens and the team can put a few ideas down on paper together.

Although you might imagine that it's the art director's task to think of the images while it's the copywriter's job to come up with the headlines, straplines and slogans, this is not always necessarily the case. At this stage, producing the concept is still very much a combined effort and the copywriter is just as likely to have a great idea for a visual as the art director is; similarly, the art director is just as likely to come up with a memorable headline or catchy slogan as is the copywriter.

Often within student teams presenting ideas, someone will proudly announce 'I had this idea.' But, when you work as a team, it's important to think of every idea as 'our idea', particularly when you're presenting it. This is something that all student teams should come to terms with and accept as early as possible, so that nobody continues to seek credit for their own ideas as individuals.

A way with words: Scamps

'Scamps' is a term used to describe the initial rough sketches and visuals that are drawn up by the creative team when they are exploring different ideas. They are often loosely rendered with marker pens on layout pads.

Above
Exploring different ideas
Once briefed, the creative team will normally spend some time talking through initial thoughts and ideas, often visualising these as rough 'scamps'.
Photo: Karina Edginton-Vigus

The creative team

Above
Running the idea past the client
Running alternative concepts past
the client at an interim stage of the
ideas process is a good way to test
the water and establish which routes
are likely to be most acceptable.
It also increases the chances that
the client will like your final ideas.
Photo: Karina Edginton-Vigus

A way with words:
Tissue meetings

No, these aren't meetings where the creative team gets the tissues out and everyone starts to weep because they haven't found an idea yet – quite the reverse. These are sessions where a variety of different creative routes are presented to the client as ideas in progress, in order to engage the client in the decision-making process and get an early sense of what is likely to get approval. These sessions enable the creative team and their agency to shortlist creative routes and eventually focus in on a single campaign concept to take through to final development. Most agencies these days agree that involving the client in the process helps create a better relationship with that client, and promotes mutual trust. So in the end everyone's happy and there's no need for tears!

Taking the idea forward

When the team realise that they have generated enough ideas to run with, they will normally present these informally to the creative director, who will then make a decision as to whether a particular concept should be developed further and prepared for presentation to the client. Meetings with the account manager and other agency departments may also be necessary at this stage if there are likely to be any questions about the viability of the idea from the client's point of view, or in terms of production itself. Tissue meetings with the client may also be arranged at interim stages prior to the final presentation of ideas.

The 'big idea' for the campaign can come from the art director or the copywriter. On some occasions it may even originate from the person who happened to wander into the room at the time, spotted what you were doing and asked: 'Have you tried this…?'

The creative team

Who does what?

In the early days of advertising, art directors and copywriters worked in separate offices or locations and there was a clear demarcation of job roles between the two. Basically, the art director would draw the pictures and hand them to the copywriter who would go away and add the words. These days it's a very different story and the whole process of working together is much more synergistic. There's no reason why the art director may not contribute to the written content of the advert, just as there's no reason why the copywriter may not be involved in the art direction of it.

It is only once the final concept and ideas have been agreed that there's likely to be any division of responsibility between the creative partners. Generally speaking, the art director will be responsible for exploring different visual layouts, perspectives, photographic or illustrative styles and typography as well as making decisions about the overall look of an advert. The copywriter, meanwhile, will set about writing the body copy, script and captions, in addition to fine-tuning any headlines, straplines or slogans where required. Even these tasks, however, may be shared between the art director and the copywriter to some extent.

In the most flexible creative teams, the art director needs to be able to write copy and the copywriter art direct, as and when the occasion arises.

There may also be times when the nature of the brief or the chosen media lends itself towards more input from either the art director or the copywriter. In the case of radio for example, there are no images to art direct. The images are created in the mind of the radio listener and prompted by the combination of sound and script. Naturally, the copywriter may be expected to contribute more to the scriptwriting of a radio commercial than the art director, but this is only an extension of a concept that they will have created together as a team. Although art direction itself may not play a key role in the creation of a radio script, storylines, scenarios, characters and other aspects of planning and directing the commercial are the responsibility of both creative partners.

Which teams get the brief?

It is the creative director's task to decide which teams work on which briefs. Different advertising agencies have different systems to deal with this. In some cases, there may be more than just one team working on the same brief at any given time, depending on the availability of resources and the volume of campaigns being handled by the creative department at the time. Having more than just one team working on a brief is advantageous, as more ideas are likely to be generated. One disadvantage to having multiple teams working on a brief may arise from the fact that many teams prefer to take ownership of a campaign. Knowing that other teams are also working on a brief can reduce the motivational pressure that exists when a team knows that it's all down to them; this can obviously be a bad thing.

The creative director's decision to allocate a particular brief to a particular team may be based on a variety of reasons, such as their familiarity with the brand or the audiences for that brand, their previous experience on the account (or similar accounts), or simply their availability or workload at the time. In some cases, certain teams may find themselves working on the same account or brand on a regular basis, while other agencies may prefer to share the accounts around among different creative teams. Some teams may specialise in working with certain categories of products, while other teams may be deemed too junior to be let loose on the agency's biggest client.

The creative director oversees the allocation of creative briefs and makes the key decisions regarding which ideas are progressed and which ones are binned.

Above
Idea rejection
Some of your best ideas may get rejected. The important thing is to bounce back with even better ones!
Photo: Nik Mahon

The role of the art director

Now that we've gained a general sense of what being an art director involves, as well as an awareness of the collective responsibilities shared by the art director and copywriter team, let's turn to look more specifically at the role that the art director plays once the overall concept for the campaign has been established and approved. This is the point in a campaign when the art director will set about crafting the actual look of the advert. This is where the job of art direction really begins.

Where to begin?

To get started, an art director normally uses fast thumbnail sketches to try out different visual variations of the initial idea, changing the positioning and size of the elements on the page in order to determine the best visual combination to suit the brief at hand and the advertising objectives stated within it. Some art directors prefer to work on computers to explore alternative layouts, since tasks such as repositioning, sizing, cropping and colour variation – together with the exchange of different images, type-styles and other graphic elements – can be achieved much more quickly this way.

Once a variety of alternative layouts have been explored and, in some cases, discussed in tissue meetings, the best solutions will be worked up as finished visuals for presentation to the client.

Putting it all together

Having largely determined the general content of the campaign idea, the next creative challenge you face is how best to put together all the visual elements that collectively make up the advert. In order to do this, the art director will experiment with different visual elements, such as the size, colour and style of typography, photography and illustration, considering the emphasis of individual elements and their juxtaposition to each other on the page, and exploring the use of camera angles, lighting and special effects.

The combination and reconfiguration of these visual elements provides the art director with an infinite number of possibilities in terms of design and creative impact.

Some useful tips

The best way to start exploring different ideas and layouts is with lots of small doodles and sketches as they can be more spontaneous and are generally faster to put down. In the time it takes to boot up your computer, you can quickly capture your initial creative ideas at the moment that they arise, by hastily sketching out two or three fleeting ideas. Once a variety of different layouts have been sketched out as rough thumbnails, it's a good time to pick the most promising layouts and work these up to a higher standard on a computer, filling in all the additional visual elements in order to get a good impression of what the finished advert may look like.

The benefit of using a computer at this stage comes from the fact that many tasks, such as flopping the image, reversing out type, substituting images, colours and type-styles, and shrinking or enlarging type- or image-based elements, can be achieved quickly and with less effort. That said, some art directors still prefer to stick to working with marker pens from start to finish when visualising their ideas. One reason for this is that a hand-drawn marker-pen visual enables art directors to visualise exactly what they have in their head. A computer visual can often compromise that original vision of the idea if the exact image is unavailable.

Above
Quick thumbnail sketches and 'one-stroke' visuals
Quick thumbnail sketches are often the best way to experiment with alternative layouts.
Photo: Nik Mahon

Working with the specialists and seeing the job through

After the idea has been approved by the client, the art director's role switches to one involving the production of the advertising campaign. This begins with the task of making sure that the right specialists are hired for the job. In terms of image production, a decision will have already been made over the medium to be used; photography, illustration, or a combination of both perhaps? Either way, the art director will decide on which photographers or illustrators to use and will subsequently brief on the assignment. These specialists will normally be selected from a collection of catalogues, portfolios, websites and database entries that the creative team have access to. Portfolios and catalogues are frequently sent in by the specialists themselves or their agents.

Selecting the right people for the job

The decision over who to choose for the job can rest on several factors. Many art directors will, over the years, have built up strong working relationships with certain photographers and illustrators, and in that time developed a good understanding and knowledge of their individual strengths and areas of expertise. For example, one photographer may have a lot of experience photographing food, whilst another may have a wealth of skill and expertise in working with children or animals. Similarly, one illustrator may have a reputation for detailed technical illustration; whilst another may have a unique talent for emulating the paintings of the old masters. If the advert requires a certain visual style or approach, then this will obviously have a bearing on which photographer or illustrator to use.

Sometimes the visual execution calls for a totally fresh or radically different treatment and so good art directors are always on the lookout for new talent and new trendsetting styles or approaches.

Commissioning typography

Typography is another element of the advert that may call for the services of a specialist; in this instance, a typographer, of course! In many cases, art directors often have the expertise to craft the typography themselves, particularly if standard typefaces are being used in a conventional way. However, if something a bit more unusual is needed, such as the manipulation of type or a new font design, then this may require more specialist skills. In some cases, the typography may be part of the image itself and would involve very close collaboration between the art director and the typographer in order to make absolutely certain that the final execution remains faithful to the original idea.

Working with photographers and illustrators

The art director will attend photographic shoots in order to make sure that the end results match up with the original concepts. Whilst the photographer has the technical know-how to take a great picture, the final responsibility for the image produced rests with the art director and so he or she will normally want to take every measure to ensure that the picture is right. In cases where the art director is unable to attend the shoot, or feels that it's not necessary, the photographer will normally be provided with a thorough briefing on what's needed, together with good visuals to work from and clear instructions on what is required.

In the case of commissioning illustrations, it's obviously essential that the illustrator is provided with an explicit and detailed brief, which covers as much information as possible, together with style guides or examples. This is particularly necessary when the art director wants the illustration to recreate a particular look or technique. In some cases the illustrator may also provide the art director with working drawings and preliminary sketches either before or during work on the final illustration.

Working with the specialists and seeing the job through

Below
Tweaking the image
Advertising photography invariably
involves retouching or image
manipulation. This is closely
supervised by the art director.
Photo: Karina Edginton-Vigus

Right
Overseeing photography
Whether in the studio or outdoors on
location, the art director will normally
attend the photo shoot to make
sure that the final image is as close
as possible to the creative team's
original idea. This outdoor location
shoot for Green Flag car breakdown
cover (top right), resulted in the
poster pictured (bottom right), which
conveys a sense of Green Flag's 'rapid'
service in both image and headline:
'Average national response time:
30 minutes'.
Agency: EHS Brann
Client: Green Flag
Creative: Jamie Pulley
Photographer: Mike Cooper

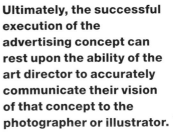

● ● ●
**Ultimately, the successful
execution of the
advertising concept can
rest upon the ability of the
art director to accurately
communicate their vision
of that concept to the
photographer or illustrator.**

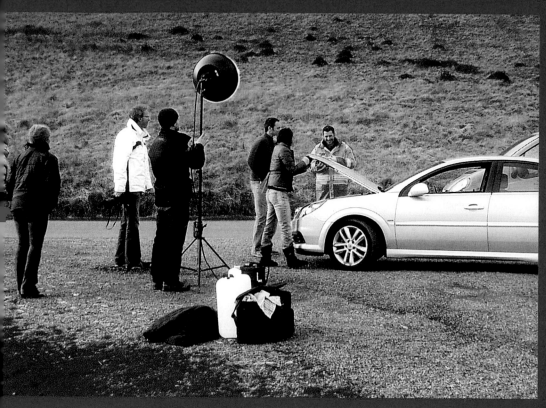

"I spy with my little eye, someth..."

AVERAGE NATIONAL RESPONSE TIME: 30 MINUTES

Green Flag
Rapid Breakdown Cover

Working with the specialists and seeing the job through

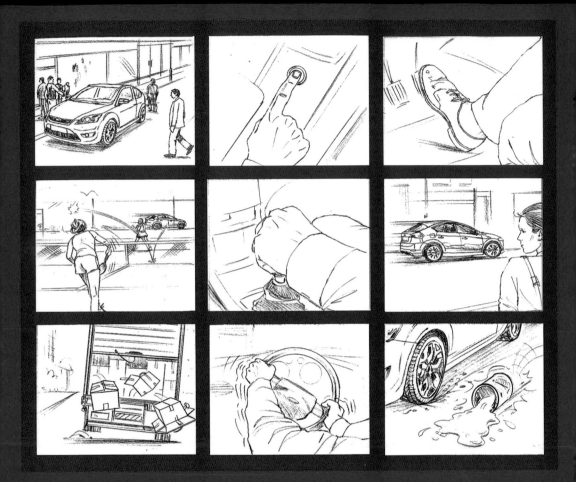

Above
The storyboard
A storyboard is a visual schedule,
mapping out the sequence of scenes
alongside the script.
Image reproduced with kind
permission of Wunderman, UK

The moving image

So far, we've concentrated on print-based advertising media, but let's not forget about advertising media that involves moving images. Where film or video footage has to be shot, the presence of the art director at the shoot is normally expected once again. If a commercial is being filmed, a commercial director will be hired to oversee the shoot and direct camerawork, lighting and the actors themselves.

Commercial directors (more commonly referred to as 'directors') come with varying degrees of experience and many of them began as art directors or copywriters themselves. For some of them, directing commercials is a stepping stone towards becoming a film director. Alan Parker's credits include *Bugsy Malone* (1976), *Midnight Express* (1978) and *The Commitments* (1991); he began his career as an advertising creative and then a commercial director, before graduating to films.

When you work with a commercial director who has this type of experience, you can normally expect him or her to contribute with further ideas and suggestions. Ultimately, as creatives themselves, they may have something to offer beyond just their expertise in directing actors, cameramen, sound and lighting. For your part, you should be open-minded enough to take their advice and suggestions on board; but at the same time, be careful that the commercial does not stray too far from your original idea. Sometimes, the technical experience and creative intuition of a good director can add something extra to the final execution of your commercial.

The role of the storyboard

When planning out a television or cinema commercial, storyboards are used to map out the sequence of scenes and the manner in which the story unfolds. Storyboards are also used to brief the commercial director and any other key members of the production team. We'll return to looking at storyboards in greater depth later in this book, but for now it's important to begin to consider their role in communicating your idea to the director and any other party involved in the production. The storyboard also enables the art director to think about the composition of the image on the screen.

Although we're talking about moving images here, the discipline of art direction remains the same, and the art director should think of each frame of film as a still image in itself.

Working with the specialists and seeing the job through

Print and production processes

In your role as art director, there are many more specialists that you will come to work with on a frequent basis: model-makers, animators, sound producers, re-touchers, image manipulators, music composers, editors, graphic designers, stylists and so on. Each of these individuals contributes their expertise to bring your idea to life; but in order to do this they will need to be well-briefed by the creative team. In many cases, the art director will be at the hub of the production process, overseeing and checking work at each stage.

Some knowledge of print and production processes is essential for all art directors, as it will have a direct bearing on what can and can't be achieved in terms of both the media (for example, press, posters, television and radio) and the medium (such as animation, illustration or photography) that is being used. For example, the absorbency of the stock that your advertisement will be printed on can have significant implications for the design. The thin, absorbent nature of newsprint stock (the technical name for the paper used in newspapers), for example, tends to result in the image bleeding slightly.

Right
Supervising production
Some basic technical knowledge in certain areas of the production process is essential. This enables the art director to have an idea of both what is, and what is not possible in terms of media and medium. Here the art director carefully examines the print proofs – a crucial part of this process.
Photo: Karina Edginton-Vigus

Fine lines and detail in general can be lost when the image is printed on newsprint, so fine serif typefaces, reversed out of a solid black background at something like 8pt in size, would probably be unreadable. Print technology has come a long way over the last decade and the advances of digital printing have done a lot to extend the capabilities of print media; however, even the most advanced printing techniques can prove to have limitations, and it is well worth being aware of these.

Printers will supply print proofs to an advertising agency prior to the full print run on any advertisement. The art director will normally be responsible for checking these proofs for details such as colour casts, poor registration or broken type. The detailed complexities of print and production processes cannot be comprehensively covered in this book, but anyone interested in a career as an art director should endeavour to gain some basic working knowledge of this area.

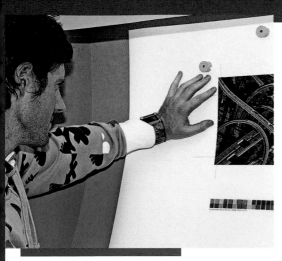

Give it a go

It's time to have a go at this yourself. By now, you should have a good idea of what art direction is and what it generally sets out to accomplish. As you're aware, art direction involves the selection and layout of the visual elements that make up an advert. This means that there are an infinite number of different ways by which any given idea or concept can be visually executed.

Choose a print advert that is currently running and examine how the different elements that make up the anatomy of the advert relate to each other in terms of size, emphasis, positioning and proximity.

Also carefully examine the use of typography, photography or illustration, together with different visual styles, camera lighting, camera angles and the selective cropping of images.

Now see if you can do a better job. Without changing the general content of the advert you're examining, have a go at experimenting with alternative layouts to improve the art direction. Bear in mind who the advert is talking to and what it's trying to say. Your art direction should help, not hinder communication. Use quick thumbnail sketches as described earlier in this chapter to test different combinations of possible layouts.

Finally, select the most promising or interesting layouts and develop them as finished visuals. When you've completed a few of these, compare them to the original advert and decide which is strongest. At this stage, don't worry if you're finding it hard to improve on the original. In the next chapter, we will explore some key tools and 'tricks' that will enable you to sharpen your art-direction skills.

2

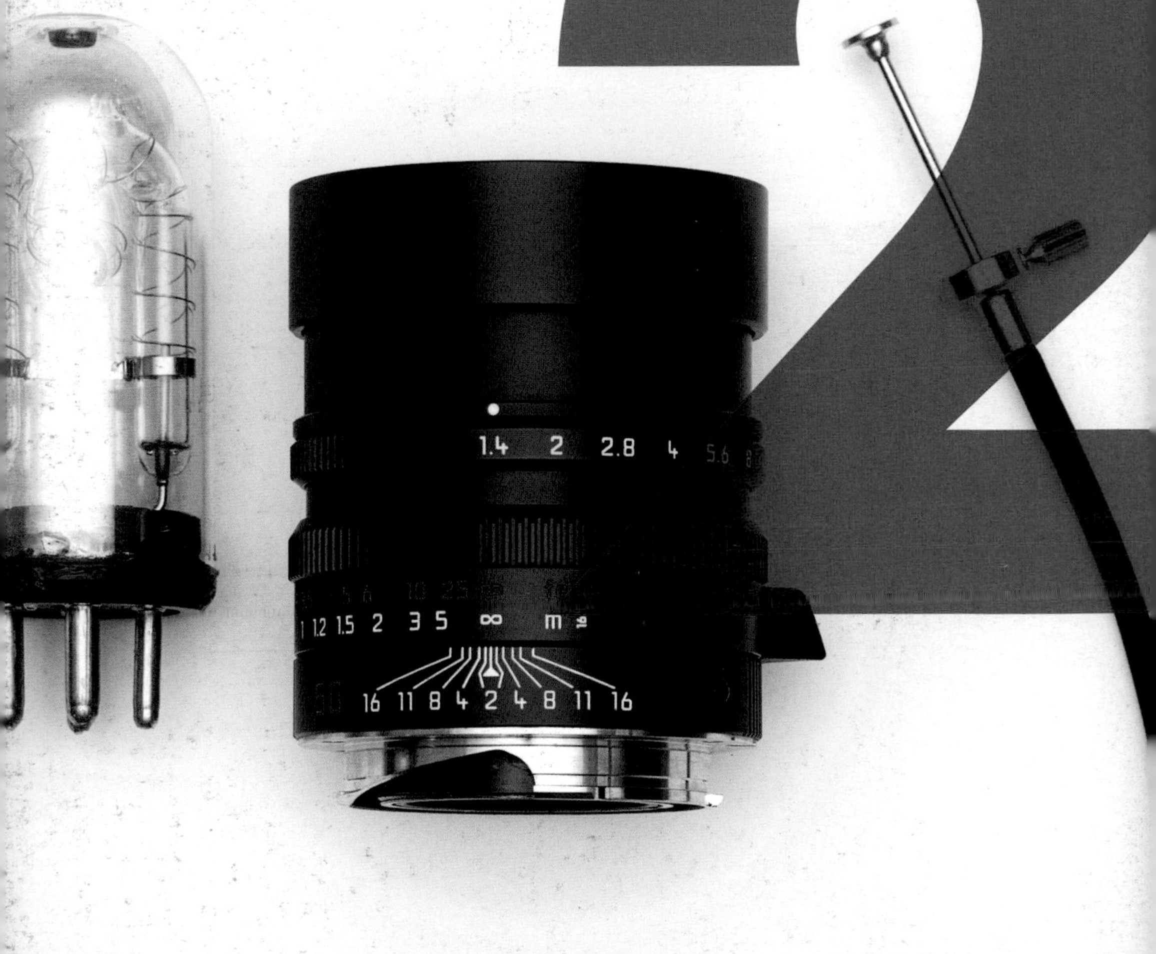

By now you should have a good idea of what art direction is and how it works.

In the first chapter of this book we looked at the wider scope of the art director's role, as one that encompasses not just the process of generating ideas and designing the layout of the advert, but one that also involves guiding and overseeing the production process at various stages.

It's now time to look at some of the 'tricks of the trade' and at the tools at your disposal.

Seeing things differently

One way to generate interest in your brand is to find a unique way of depicting it in your advert. In order to find a different or unusual way of showing either the brand, or communicating the brand proposition, you must first find a way of seeing it differently. Sometimes, the idea itself can help you with this. Occasionally, you can let the idea or even the brand proposition do the art directing for you – or at least suggest the imagery to you. For example, if the proposition says: 'Tell people that our brand will make you feel ten feet tall,' you could show a photograph taken from a high viewpoint, looking down. Alternatively, imagine how it would feel, or what you could do, or how you may act if you were ten feet tall. Is there some way you can show this in the advert?

Ultimately, you need to be asking yourself: what does the product benefit *really* mean to the target audience or end-user? If it's a deodorant for men, the proposition might be: 'You'll smell great 24 hours a day.' But what this really means to the end-user is: 'You'll be more sexually attractive!'

Looking beyond the product benefit

Sometimes it's a case of looking beyond the more obvious product benefit in order to find another way of seeing the brand. When Polaroid wanted to find a new way to promote their instant camera, they didn't simply assert the fact that it provided photographs instantly. Instead, they looked at the consequences of instant photography; one of these being that the camera would be a lot of fun at a party or other social occasion. As a result, advertising didn't focus on selling an instant camera, but a 'social lubricant'. Looking at the consequences of the product benefit in this way opens up a fresh range of alternative routes to explore.

If you're lucky, finding a different way to present a product may simply be a case of exploring different angles of view or different ways of placing that product in front of the camera lens. The beauty of an idea can often be in its simplicity.

Turning the product on its head

In Canada, advertising agency Ogilvy & Mather had the task of revitalising the breakfast cereal brand Shreddies. The brand image was seen as 'tired' and boring in comparison to some of the newer breakfast cereals on the market. In a single stroke of creative genius a 26-year-old intern at the agency had the idea of relaunching the brand as new 'Diamond-shaped Shreddies'. Of course, the cereal hadn't really changed at all. All the agency had done was to rotate the regular square-shaped piece of cereal *en pointe* to create a diamond shape that subsequently appeared on all packaging, advertising and other promotional media.

The new diamond-shaped Shreddies were launched in 2008, generating dramatic increase in sales of the product and prompting internet blogs, discussion groups, forums, rants and an unprecedented level of media hype for the once humble cereal. Focus groups were orchestrated by the agency to discuss the merits of the new diamond-shape variety, and many swore that yes – you can taste the difference! One enterprising individual even placed what he claimed to be the last surviving square Shreddie on eBay, selling it off for the grand sum of US$36.

Above
Turning the product on its head
In Canada, the agency Ogilvy & Mather revitalised the breakfast cereal Shreddies by simply turning the square-shaped pieces of cereal *en-pointe* to create new 'diamond'-shaped Shreddies. Old 'square' Shreddies or new, exciting 'diamond-shaped' Shreddies – which would you prefer?
Photo: © David Shaw

Seeing things differently

Some useful tips

One method to explore all of the different ways that you can show the product or brand is by asking a series of questions or prompts. Can I substitute something else for the product (perhaps a metaphor for the product)? Can I combine or compare it with something else or add something to it? Can I adapt it in some way? Can I show it bigger or smaller? Can I show lots of images of the product? Can I show just a part of it? Can I deconstruct it in some way (perhaps show all of its component parts)? Can I show it from a different angle or point of view?

All of these questions can serve as prompts that you can use to stimulate alternative ways of visually presenting the product or brand. You can probably add your own questions to this list. Ultimately, you should be exploring different ways of showing your client's brand that demonstrate or highlight the benefit of it, or of its advertising message, in an original and memorable way.

Making the familiar *unfamiliar*

Perhaps one of the most challenging tasks for the art director is to present images of everyday products or familiar brands in fresh, surprising ways. The trick is to make the usual *unusual*, the familiar *unfamiliar* and the ordinary *extraordinary*. Ask yourself what else the product could be to your audience (or how else could you show the product)?

One method of visually presenting a familiar image in an unfamiliar and more interesting way is to 'zoom-in' close on one element of detail, effectively magnifying it and cropping the full image. This can sometimes result in an image that isn't immediately recognisable or takes on the appearance of something else. In other cases, closing in on the detail can draw the audience's attention to an aspect of the product that they had not previously appreciated or observed for themselves.

By presenting the product
(or an image associated
with the product) in an
unfamiliar way, you can
grab attention with a
picture that is visually more
interesting or intriguing.

Below
Closing in on the detail
The close-up image in this advert
for Howies draws attention to the
detail that goes into the design of
their jeans and presents an
ordinary, everyday product in a
striking, unexpected manner. At the
same time, the underlying message
conveyed is that this is a high-quality
product, the ad making reference to
the 'angled belt loops' of their jeans.
Agency: Dye Holloway Murray
Art Director: Dave Dye
Client: Howies
Copywriter: Dave Dye
Creative Director: Dave Dye
Photographer: Laurence Haskell

Angled belt loops.
They allow you to put your belt
through 0.6 seconds quicker.
Though if you're looking to gain
that extra time, it may be worth
looking at other areas of your life
aside from getting dressed.

howies.co.uk

Reframing

Presenting a product from a different perspective, or causing your audience to redefine their perception of the product (or something associated with the product), is another means by which clever art direction can create an element of visual surprise. In some cases, it can be the headline, strapline, body-copy or even the logo that can turn the initial interpretation of an image on its head. At other times, it may be the image itself that changes the meaning of the headline. This process is called *reframing* and it occurs when an element of the communication, such as a line of copy or an image, changes the subsequent interpretation of that communication.

Reframing operates on the fundamental principle that we interpret sensory information based on our previous knowledge and experience – or frame of reference. As we start to receive that information, we locate a frame of reference to give meaning to it, and to make sense of it. In other words, we contextualise the information at the outset.

When the reframing element is introduced (typically with a print ad, this will be a headline, logo or image), this conflicts with our initial frame of reference and an alternative interpretation presents itself. To put it simply: when the context changes, the meaning changes also.

Time-based media such as radio, television and cinema can sometimes provide a more effective media platform for reframing, as the reframing element can remain hidden until the right moment.

There is a greater opportunity for the creative team to deliberately confound the expectations of the listener or viewer by establishing a frame of reference through the use of stereotypes, clichés, recognised routines or behaviour. This frame of reference is then overturned by a single line of script or an unexpected moment. For example, imagine the opening frames of a TV commercial depicting a head-and-shoulders frame of a tough-looking, leather-clad biker, with a shaven, tattooed head, several conspicuous body piercings to his face and several missing teeth. Then imagine that the camera zooms back to reveal him reading a romantic paperback novel and the voiceover exclaims: 'Supersoft toilet paper can bring out the softer side in anyone.' It's all about surprise. In order to surprise your audience, you first have to know what they expect to hear or see… then you do the opposite!

The key to reframing is to first establish how your audience will initially interpret what is happening in your advert or commercial. Certain words, terms and images will often trigger predictable thoughts and responses, and so you can use these to guide audience expectations in one direction, before turning those expectations around.

Above

Shifting perspective to reframe what we see

In the first scene from this commercial for *The Guardian* newspaper in the UK, we see a young man running desperately down the street. His general demeanour, dress and overall appearance suggest that he's been involved in some kind of trouble. In the next scene, the camera viewpoint changes and we see the young man struggling to take a briefcase from an older gentleman – or so it would appear.

In the final scene, however, the camera angle changes once more to give us an aerial view looking down to see a mass of construction materials from the adjacent building, tumbling down towards them. The younger man is in fact saving the older man's life. The advertising message aims to suggest that *The Guardian* newspaper provides the 'whole story'. When the camera viewpoint changes, the frame of reference shifts, as does our interpretation of what we see.
Agency: DDB London
Client: The Guardian

Seeing things differently

We were going to ask Bonington to take
our cameras up Everest, but he asked us first.

To see what the smallest, lightest SLR cameras in the world can do, turn to the cover and pages 44–51 of the Colour Magazine. For information about Olympus OM2 cameras write to Dept. ST1, Olympus Optical Co. (U.K.) Ltd., 5–9 Glasshouse Yard, London EC1A 4JP.

Facing page
Using words to reframe images
In these adverts for the Volkswagen Golf
car, the contradiction between what we
see in the photograph, and what we read
in the one-word headline confounds our
expectations and causes us to question
why a tiny tropical island should be 'Hell'
and a nightmarish meandering mountain
road, 'Heaven'. The Golf VW logo in the
bottom right-hand corner reframes
the context of the image and reveals why!
The contrast between the dramatic imagery
of the photographs and the understated
typography adds to the visual 'tease'.
Agency: Ogilvy & Mather
Art Director: Jonathan Lang
Client: Volkswagen of South Africa
Creative Director: Dave Dye
Images used courtesy of Ogilvy Cape Town
and Volkswagen South Africa

Left
**Finding a different way to show
the product**
The clever positioning of product and
person, together with the high contrast,
grainy, monochromatic finish of the print,
combine to create an unusual and dramatic,
alien-like image of mountain climber,
Chris Bonington, using his Olympus
camera. Man and machine merge,
depicting the camera as an extension of
the photographer himself.
Client: Olympus
Photographer: Barney Edwards
Image: © Barney Edwards at Lens Modern

Seeing things differently

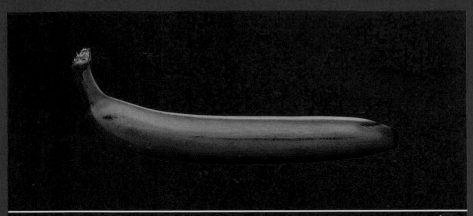

Virgin HOLIDAYS   Manchester direct to Barbados.   virgin atlantic Virgin

قريبا

DUBAI. From 27 March.   virgin atlantic Virgin

4 flights a week from March, 5 from May. Daily from June.

Banana
Agency: RKCR/ Y&R
Client: Virgin Atlantic
Photographer: Paul Zak
Soon
Agency: RKCR/ Y&R
Client: Virgin Atlantic

Above
**Could the product look like
something else?**
Subtle photo-manipulation of a
banana and creative rendering
of an Arabic typeface allude to the
image of an aircraft fuselage, whilst
providing a visual reference to the
flight destinations (Barbados, top;
Dubai, bottom) that are being featured
in these posters for Virgin Atlantic.

Other ways of creating unusual images

By placing your client's product in situations of which the audience have no personal knowledge or experience, you have further opportunities to use unusual imagery to communicate with that audience. It's also worth considering whether to show the product in pristine 'out-of-the-box' condition, or alternatively, whether it may in fact prove more interesting to show what the product looks like when it's being used, perhaps in extreme circumstances or conditions.

One way of creating a remarkable image is to look at how the product, an aspect or detail of it, or something related to it, could look like something else when seen from a different angle or viewpoint. Sometimes, you can add detail or manipulate the image in a subtle way to help communicate the advertising message.

In all cases, you should be attempting to avoid the 'same old shot' (SOS) syndrome. Think of the most common advertising images that are used to promote the product genre – then create something that's totally different.

Give it a go

Choose one of the following generic products and consider the different ways that you can show each of them or demonstrate a product benefit: a mobile phone; a pair of stereo headphones; a pair of rugged walking boots; an electric lawnmower, or low-fat sausages.

First, experiment with the different viewpoints, possible camera angles, close-up detail and what the product looks like if you modify or adapt it in some way. Think also about the different ways that the product is, or could be, used – and the different people that may use it and the different situations or places *where* they may use it. Consider how the product may change in appearance as a result of how it is used or even misused.

On some occasions, it may be more interesting not to show the product, but to focus instead on the effects of the product. In all cases, look for the unusual, dramatic or unexpected shot.

Sketch out or photograph your image ideas. At this stage, don't worry too much about headlines, straplines or logos unless they're an integral part of your idea. Focus mainly on the image.

Doing things differently

One word that has already emerged several times in this book is 'surprise'. The capacity to surprise your audience is a fundamental component of creative advertising. Whilst the ability to see and present familiar objects or images in different and unusual ways is one method of creating surprise, another way is to confound the expectations of the audience through the execution of the idea. In order to do this, you have to first establish what kind of things the target audience expect to see, or normally associate with the subject area or product that is being advertised. Then it's simply a case of doing something that's different. The tricky bit is doing something that's different, but at the same time relevant to the advertising message.

From unusual images to unusual use of media

One way of presenting the brand in a different way is to first identify generic imagery, visual themes, style of photography, tone of voice, terminology, and the style of language normally associated with similar brands or products. Then try to create a series of visual ideas that break these stereotypes. There is an intrinsic quality of 'sameness' evident in most of the advertising material we see about us today. Most car adverts look like car adverts, most mobile phone commercials look like mobile phone commercials, most hair-care and beauty campaigns look like hair-care and beauty campaigns and so on…. So, as soon as we start to do something unexpected with the way that we present the visual material, we start to grab the audience's attention.

Another way of executing the idea in an unusual manner is to do something different with the media itself. Think of the conventional ways in which the various media are used, and consider doing something unconventional. For example: why do 48-sheet billboards have to be landscape format – can you turn them on their end as long, tall posters? Do magazine adverts have to be printed on the same stock as the rest of the magazine? Are there any other, more unusual forms of media where your adverts can be placed? Remember that your aim in all of this is to grab attention in a surprising and unexpected manner that is relevant to the brand and the message being communicated – the brand proposition.

Right
Using the media in an amazing way
This poster stunt featured a dramatic demonstration of just how strong Araldite glue is. The humorous and clever headlines used in the ads testified to the strength of the glue ('It also sticks handles to teapots'; 'The tension mounts'; 'How did we pull it off?'), as well as to the novel poster campaign itself. Extraordinary use of the media grabbed the public's attention and got people talking about the campaign long before the term 'viral advertising' had been coined.
Agency: FCO Univas, London
Art Directors: Rob Kitchen, Ian Potter
Client: Araldite
Copywriter: Rob Janowski
Images courtesy of the Advertising Archives

● ● ●

Be creative in the way in which you use the chosen advertising media. Ask yourself if there's anything unusual that you can do with the media that will help to underline the key advertising message.

Doing things differently

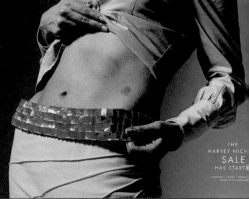

Give it a go

Take a look at some of the latest advertising campaigns for *hair-care* or *beauty* products. Generally speaking, and with few exceptions, they all tend to use the same look and visual style even though they may be emphasising different product benefits and features. In other words, they all look like hair-care and beauty adverts are expected to look.

Now is your chance to do the unexpected. Choose a current advert or commercial from this category. Next, identify who the target market are and what the advertising proposition is. Now re-do the advert or commercial in the style of one of the following: an *army recruitment* advert; a *beer* advert; or an advert for a *car*. Alternatively, choose any other category of advertising to emulate in terms of style – just as long as you find a way to make the choice of style unconventional yet relevant to the advertising message.

Left

Victims of violence, or victims of fashion?

What appears at first to be a campaign raising the issue of domestic violence is revealed to be no more than a series of posters announcing that the sale at Harvey Nichols has started. The conflict between the image and the copyline is resolved when we make the connection between the injuries depicted and the Harvey Nichols sale (the real cause of the injuries). The apparent brutality of the imagery, the anonymity of the female model and the gloomy monochromatic lighting all contribute to our misperception of the subject matter and subsequently enhance the reframing effect when the real advertising message is revealed.

Agency: BMP DDB London
Art Director: Justin Tindall
Client: Harvey Nichols
Copywriter: Adam Tucker
Creative Director: Mark Reddy
Photographer: Ben Stockley
Typographer: Kevin Clarke
Images: © Ben Stockley

Give the audience something to discover

Some of the best adverts give the audience something to discover for themselves. In some cases, this may simply involve the recognition of a 'double meaning' when headline and image are viewed together. In other cases, it may involve hidden symbolism or a brand message concealed beneath the surface. Either way, some level of decoding on the part of the audience is required.

Remember that if the advert requires very little or no thought on the part of the audience, then you're missing an opportunity to engage or interact with that audience.

The media-literate audience

There is an old-fashioned notion that if the audience doesn't 'get' your advert instantly, then it isn't working. This may have been the case back in the 1960s when advertising audiences were generally passive consumers of the media, but today's media-literate audiences tend to relate on a more interactive level with the advertising that they are confronted with. That's not to say that you can get away with adverts that are wantonly cryptic or confusing; it's just a case of crediting your audience with an appropriate level of intelligence and curiosity.

Obviously, the advertising message has to be understood by your audience, even if that understanding isn't instant. Today, audiences are generally more readily willing and able to search for hidden meanings, to make metaphorical connections and to unravel the advertising message from what they see. They can do this because they have a greater understanding of the language of advertising than their predecessors had. They are media savvy and tend to engage with advertising to a much greater extent, and at a higher level than in the past. This factor, combined with the natural inclination of human beings to solve puzzles and resolve ambiguous information, provides today's advertisers with a great opportunity to develop a more interactive relationship with their audiences through advertising communication.

Above
Making your audience look again
An unusual image can prompt your
audience to 'look twice'. These
images, advertising Levi's 'classic
men's 501' jeans, '…now re-cut
for women', depict a young man and
woman whose limbs are morphed
together in such a fashion that
it's not clear whether the image
has been manipulated or just
cleverly photographed.
Agency: Bartle Bogle Hegarty
Asia Pacific
Art Director: Alex Lim Thye Aun
Client: Levi Strauss Japan
Copywriter: Marthinus Strydom
Creative Director: Steve Elrick
Photographer: Nadav Kander
Images: © Nadav Kandar

Allowing the audience to make the connection

The creative execution of the advert should
provide just enough information to allow
the audience to make the connection and
to understand its implicit message. Making
the message too obvious can reduce the
memorability and general impact of the idea;
whilst something that's too obscure will
never be understood. At the same time,
don't expect your audience to interpret the
diffused glow in the top right-hand corner
of your advert as symbolising humanity's
struggle in a post-modernist society for
a better future in a world that's bereft of
understanding and compassion – that's
best left to books or academic papers
on semiotics! Whilst certain images
or references can work on a more
subconscious level, the basic advertising
proposition has to be a lot clearer than that.

'Getting' an advert is a bit like 'getting' a
joke. The joke is funnier if you have to think
about it for a while. We've all witnessed the
spontaneous outburst of laughter from
the person who 'gets' the joke a few minutes
after everyone else in the room. It's as though
the delay has resulted in a greater effect.

Ultimately, when it comes down to your
advert, you have to know how much
information to feed your audience, and
how much to hold back in order to enable
them to make the connection themselves.
If the audience are left with no connection
to make, and nothing to discover for
themselves, then the chances are that the
advert will be forgotten in no time. This is
where clever art direction and copywriting
comes into play.

Give the audience something to discover

Left
Making your audience look again, and again...
This advert for Levi's 501 jeans was one of several from the same campaign as that featured previously (see page 57). Once again, it employs visual ambiguity as a key aspect of the art direction.
Agency: Bartle Bogle Hegarty Asia-Pacific
Art Director: Alex Lim Thye Aun
Client: Levi Strauss Japan
Copywriter: Marthinus Strydom
Creative Director: Steve Elrick
Photographer: Nadav Kander
Images: © Nadav Kander

Above
Making your audience look more closely
It takes a few seconds for us to see what's happening in this image, but when we do, the remarkable properties of Tide clothes washing tablets are communicated in a novel, witty and impactful way. Clever art direction compels us to search for the visual clues that allow us to make sense of this advert.
Agency: Saatchi & Saatchi
Art Director: J. Jacobs
Client: Procter & Gamble
Creative Director: T. Granger
Product: Tide

Using ambiguous imagery

We've noted so far the importance of allowing the audience to make their own connections and discoveries; and the fact that providing the advertising proposition is clearly communicated, it doesn't really matter if the audience have had to think about it for a while – it's often better that way. However, as with all rules in advertising, there are moments when breaking those rules can prove to be both opportunistic and timely. On some occasions, you may find that it's ambiguity rather than clarity that gets your target audience talking or thinking about the brand. Some of the best examples of ambiguous advertising imagery can be found amongst the archives of major tobacco brands, who were forced to develop alternative creative strategies in response to government legislation in the United Kingdom.

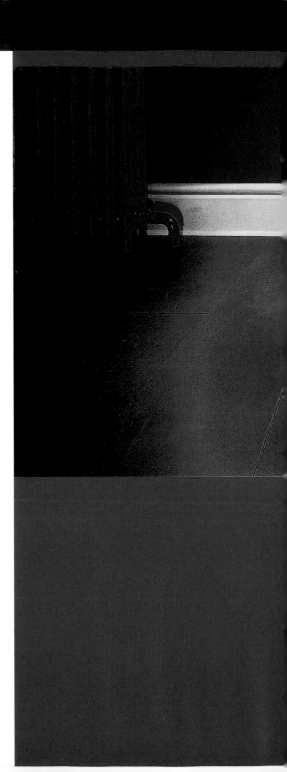

Agency: Collett Dickenson Pearce
(CDP)
Art Director: Alan Waldie
Brand: Benson & Hedges
Client: Gallaher
Photographer: Brian Duffy
Images reproduced
with kind permission of
Collett Dickenson Pearce

Above
**Visual conundrums that engage
us with the brand**
A mouse. A cat, a piece of cheese, or a
mousetrap? Oh... and spot the hidden
cigarette in this print advert produced
for cigarette brand Benson & Hedges.

Using ambiguous imagery

From pyramids to *Psycho* – how ambiguity stimulates the imagination

Back in the 1970s, the advertising agency Collett Dickenson Pearce (CDP) produced the first of many surreal, print-based adverts for Benson & Hedges cigarettes (see page 60). The advert featured the gold cigarette pack poised outside a mousehole. The rather obscure nature of this advert was CDP's response to new government legislation in the UK at that time, restricting the use of any references to high status, sexual attractiveness, celebrities, young people, power, authority or any other areas that were traditionally used by brands to create positive associations in cigarette advertising. The image itself was reported to have been inspired by a book on French surrealist photography, and spawned a succession of similarly styled adverts for the brand over the years that followed. The use of this ambiguous image raises several questions: Why the mousehole? What does the pack symbolise? What is the relevance of this imagery? What are Benson & Hedges trying to say?

The fact is, ambiguous information ultimately stimulates our imagination. We will naturally read all kinds of interpretations and hidden meanings into it. To some of us, the pack will represent cheese; to others, a mousetrap; whilst another person may see the pack as representing a waiting cat or predator. Twenty different people may have 20 unique interpretations of the image, which obviously symbolises something – but what, exactly?

The real craft of art direction in all of these examples lies in the almost intuitive skill of knowing exactly how many visual clues or references to incorporate into an advert. Once again, it's all about allowing your audience to make their own discoveries and find their own connections.

It's part of our nature to try to find meaning in ambiguous information, to resolve conundrums. And so it follows that when we're presented with this advert we'll spend some time trying to work out what exactly is going on. All the time we're doing this, the brand image is constantly being embedded in our consciousness. You could call it 'branding by stealth'! By the way, did you spot the hidden cigarette in the poster (on pages 60–61)? (Look at where the skirting board meets the carpet, running from the mousehole to the bottom edge of the image.)

The use of surrealism and ambiguity was developed further by Silk Cut, another brand of cigarettes from Gallaher (the same manufacturer as that of Benson & Hedges). This time, the agency responsible for the advertising was Saatchi & Saatchi.

The first advert in this series was a colour poster appearing in 1983, depicting a length of purple silk with a knife or scissor slash running across it – a visual pun on the brand name. This image established the theme for the print campaigns that followed, each suggesting the brand name through the use of symbolism and visual references in an increasingly ambiguous and cryptic fashion. Images used ranged from that of a Venus flytrap plant chewing on the torn crotch section from a pair of silk trousers, to a purple shower curtain alluding to the infamous shower scene in the Alfred Hitchcock film, *Psycho*.

The pervading themes of violence, sex, death and danger that appeared to characterise much of the imagery used by Silk Cut (and to some extent by Benson & Hedges) were not lost on those interested in the semiotic language of advertising. The use of ambiguous imagery in advertising can, when used appropriately, stimulate your audience's imagination and generate discussion and debate beyond the advertising itself. This, in turn, can help raise both the profile and familiarity of the brand and can be achieved in a manner that is fun and entertaining for your audience.

Of course, today there is a complete ban on cigarette advertising in the United Kingdom. However, this doesn't lessen the creative genius of those advertisements from the past; and their use of ambiguous imagery provides an excellent template for other products and brands today.

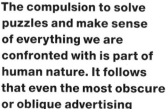

The compulsion to solve puzzles and make sense of everything we are confronted with is part of human nature. It follows that even the most obscure or oblique advertising messages can engage us in a dialogue with the brand and so promote interaction.

Using ambiguous imagery

LOW TAR As defined by H.M. Government
Warning: SMOKING CAN CAUSE LUNG CANCER, BRONCHITIS AND OTHER CHEST DISEASES
Health Departments' Chief Medical Officers

MIDD
H.M. Government Health Departments' WA

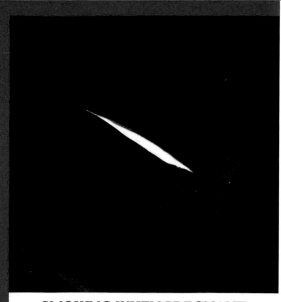

SMOKING WHEN PREGNANT
HARMS YOUR BABY

Chief Medical Officers' Warning
5mg Tar   0.5mg Nicotine

Left
Slashed silk and slasher movies!
Simple visual puns or dark
Freudian symbolism and hidden
meanings? Silk Cut used visual puns
on the brand name to entertain and
engage their audience. As each
advert became more abstract and
ambiguous, it presented more of a
challenge to decrypt and interpret the
hidden narrative.
Agency: Saatchi & Saatchi
Brand: Silk Cut
Client: Gallaher
Creatives: Paul Arden, Charles Saatchi
Images courtesy of the
Advertising Archives

Below left
**How ambiguity can
strengthen branding**
At first glance, we see four pyramids.
On closer inspection, we realise
that the pyramid in the background
is actually a Benson & Hedges
cigarette pack. This is very clever
art direction, which provides a
moment of discovery. The ambiguous
image presents us with a conundrum
to solve; and while we're trying to
solve it, the image of the gold Benson
& Hedges pack is being branded in
our thoughts. Ownership of the colour
gold established a surreal campaign
theme that sustained a strong brand
image for Benson & Hedges, in the
late 1970s through to the 1980s.
Agency: Collett Dickenson Pearce
(CDP)
Art Director: Neil Godfrey
Brand: Benson & Hedges
Client: Gallaher
Photographer: Jimmy Wormser
Images reproduced
with kind permission of
Collett Dickenson Pearce

M Government
TTES CAN SERIOUSLY DAMAGE YOUR HEALTH

Establishing a visual hierarchy

One of the most essential tasks involved in art directing print-based advertising is to create a visual hierarchy in the design and layout of the advert. In plain terms, this means placing more visual emphasis on certain elements over others, in order to establish a running order in which these elements are seen or perceived when the advert is initially viewed. It also involves making sure that key elements aren't competing for attention, but instead work together to ensure that the storyline or scenario unfolds in the right sequence to reveal the advertising message at the right moment.

Guiding the eye of the reader through the advert in a predictable sequence of perceived visual elements is a key skill that enables the art director to deliver the advertising message in an unexpected and impactful manner, at the right moment.

The order in which the elements are seen

In most print-based adverts, the first thing the viewer sees is the main image, closely followed by the headline. The next element is the logo and strapline followed by any inset images and captions. The very last thing the viewer will do is read the body copy; and if the advert hasn't interested them up to that point, they won't even bother doing that. With the knowledge that the image, headline, logo and strapline often have to tell a story without the aid of the body copy, careful consideration has to be given to the manner in which these elements relate to each other on the page. I should add that there will often be occasions where, in order for the advert to work, the art director needs people to read the headline first, before they look at the image.

Using visual hierarchy to create surprise

Establishing a visual hierarchy in your art direction consolidates some of the principles already discussed in this chapter. First, it allows reframing to occur – something that's not always easy in print-based media. Once you've mastered the ability to direct the sequence in which your audience will view the visual elements in the advert, you can place the 'revealing' moment at the end of that sequence, in order to take your audience by surprise. It's a classic case of reframing, where the context of what your audience initially sees is changed by what transpires as they read on.

Secondly, a well-considered visual hierarchy allows your audience to make their own 'discoveries' (even though these discoveries are pre-determined and engineered by your art direction). The meanings that your audience draw from your advert will require them to piece together all of the visual information and make their own connections and deductions. The sense of discovery that your audience will feel when they understand the meaning of what they see should be both impactful and rewarding.

Sometimes the 'surprise effect' can be heightened by showing the audience something at the outset that you know they won't really see or perceive at first glance. This could be something that the audience have to quite literally search or scan the advert closely for. Alternatively, it could be something that is clearly visible, but which takes on a new meaning as the story unfolds.

Creating contrast between the visual elements

There are a few rules of thumb to bear in mind when you are combining elements on the page to establish a visual hierarchy. Generally speaking, if you have a bold, dramatic image, or an image where there's a lot of visual information for the audience to absorb, it's often best to contrast this with a 'quietly spoken' piece of understated typography for the headline. You don't want the headline to be shouting out loud if the picture is already doing this. And vice versa: if the headline is already doing all the 'shouting', then it's often best to contrast this with a simple visual, such as a small 'cut-out' image, or inset photograph. Of course, sometimes there may be no image or no headline, in which case the element that provides counterpoint and meaning to the image will instead be the logo or strapline t is important to make certain that the visual elements complement each other. If all of these elements have visual equity, and there is no emphasis on a single one, then there's nothing to grab the attention of your audience. In these circumstances, the appearance of the advert can be very 'busy' – with typography, photography, illustration, headlines, straplines, logos and captions all competing against each other for the attention of the audience.

Overall, only one visual element should be dominating the page, and the extent to which it does that will depend on the idea itself and the manner in which the art direction can best communicate that idea.

Establishing a visual hierarchy

My mom's
going to
kill me.

My mom's
going to
kill me.

One condom
saves both lives.
Save the Children.

Left
Allowing a story to unfold
This advert for the charitable
organisation, Save the Children,
'ticks all the boxes': simplicity,
unexpectedness and an economy
of visual elements whose
well-considered hierarchy allows a
story to unfold, revealing itself only
at the last moment as we read the
final piece of copy. After the image
of the girl has grabbed our attention,
we read the first part of the copy:
'My Mom's going to kill me.' Our eyes
follow the bodyline of the girl, to read
the second part of the copy, which
is strategically placed alongside her
belly and repeats the first: 'My Mom's
going to kill me.' The reframing is
complete when we read the last part
of the copy together with the strapline:
'One condom saves both lives.'
Suddenly, the context changes and
the image takes on a new meaning.
Agency: BBDO Atlanta
Art Directors: Jessica Foster,
Rich Wakefield
Client: Save the Children
Copywriter: Jean Weisman
Creative Directors: Bill Pauls,
Rich Wakefield
Model: Elite Atlanta
Photographer: Jim Fiscus
Image: © Jim Fiscus

The rather spacious Golf Estate.

Above
Using a visual hierarchy
The first elements we are drawn to
are the 'lost dog' poster and the car.
Then we cast our eyes to the bottom
right-hand corner of the advert to read
the copyline that accompanies the VW
logo: 'The rather spacious Golf Estate'.
Finally, we spot the lost pet staring
out from the back of the window in the
back of the 'rather spacious' car. The
product benefit is underlined in a witty
manner, with a clever and deliberate
use of visual hierarchy.
Agency: BMP DDB London
Art Director: Ed Morris
Client: Volkswagen Group
Photographer: Kiran Master

Creating visual impact

Creating visual impact is ultimately about grabbing attention in a manner that is relevant to the advertising message. An advert with good visual impact can create a profound effect on the viewer. There are several ways in which you can create this impact. Earlier in this chapter, we looked at some of these approaches; such as the use of unfamiliar subject material, or alternatively, the use of familiar subject material made unfamiliar by the manner or context in which it is filmed, photographed or illustrated. Alternatively, you can experiment with the design layout of the advert itself and the relationship between the different visual elements. Finally, there's the advertising media and the different and unusual ways that you can use it to create that impact.

Using compelling images

Some images are more compelling than others. These may include images that are shocking, poignant, heart-warming, thought-provoking, topical, or simply unusual in a variety of other respects. In many cases, they are images that interest us because of the subject matter. There are certain topics that are guaranteed to generate interest depending on the target audience. News images are a good example of this.

Photojournalists understand the importance of newsworthy images that depict scenes of topical interest. These scenes can involve a range of different subjects, from celebrities and politicians, to road traffic accidents and global disasters. The level of interest your image may (or may not) generate is greatly dependent on the interests and issue orientation of the audience, but there are certain subjects that are generally compelling for most audiences.

Although depicting unusual subject matter can give you a headstart towards grabbing attention, remember also that even the most common, everyday items and subjects can look unusual and be just as visually compelling when new ways of presenting them are fully explored. There's no such thing as a dull product. However, there is such a thing as dull advertising: be different!

Images of disaster, for example, can appeal to our morbid sense of curiosity. Similarly, scenes involving birth, death or other states of the human condition that we are not used to seeing, will often have a certain voyeuristic quality and are more likely to grab attention and draw the reader into your advert. When you are depicting such scenes, it is important to treat them with an appropriate level of sensitivity, particularly if you are showing, or referring to, real people. Whilst a newspaper may use such images to sell more newspapers, as an art director, you don't want to end up annoying or alienating your client's target audience. It's often good to be provocative, but you have to first decide what it is that you want to provoke – that's where the creative brief should help you.

Exploring unusual layout and design

Looking for fresh and unusual formats in terms of layout and design is a key skill when it comes to creating visual impact. This is where other aspects of art direction such as the 'visual hierarchy' and contrast between design elements become important; but a simple guideline to follow is to look at what similar products are doing, and to do something different. Avoid layouts that are obvious or 'expected'. Above all, be bold in your design. This doesn't mean that your image has to 'scream out loud' from the page. It's more about taking a risk by creating something that's very different from the norm and hasn't been seen, tried or tested before. At the same time, have a good reason to be different – ultimately you'll have to justify the decisions that you make.

Visual impact is created by a combination of *what* you choose to show in your advert and *how* you choose to show it. Sometimes, the layout of the visual material itself can be compelling enough to draw the viewer into the headline or body copy, but it needs to stand out from all of the other adverts for similar products or services that generally tend to look the same and follow the 'rules' of what an advert for that product category should look like. This is your chance to break the rules!

Creating visual impact

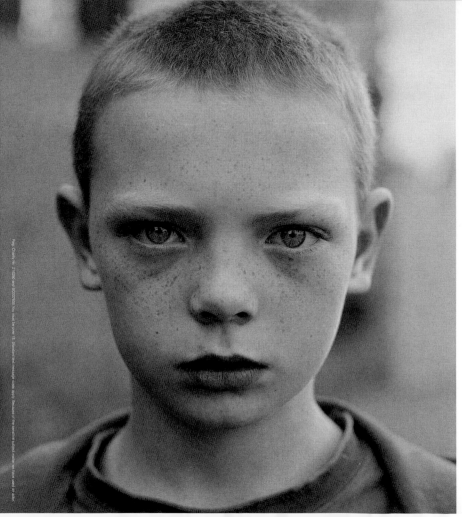

He told
his parents
to f**k off.
He told his
foster
parents
to f**k off.
He told
fourteen
social
workers
to f**k off.
He told
us to
f**k off.
But we
didn't.
And we
still haven't.

There are thousands
of disadvantaged
children in the UK.
Many of them have
stories that would
break your heart.
Some of them are
capable of terrible
things. But if,
like us, you believe
that no child is born
bad, then you can't
watch someone get
dumped into the file
marked 'problem'.
You can't let society
play pass the parcel
with a young
person's life. If a
child is referred
to Barnardo's
we stick by that
child. We listen.
We look for potential.
We give practical
support. And if we
don't give up on the
troubled, young boy,
it's not because we
enjoy being sworn at,
it's because we
believe in him.

**Believe in
children
🏠 Barnardo's**

To show you
believe in children,
text 'Believe'
to 84862 or visit
barnardos.org.uk

Left
Finding a compelling image
Even the stare of a human face can be
visually compelling, particularly when
it's communicating extreme emotions
that entice you to read the copy. The
drama and visual dominance of the
image in this advert for Barnardo's
is contrasted with the understated
typography that commences with a
suitably 'hard-hitting' headline: 'He
told his parents to f**k off. He told
his foster parents to f**k off. He told
fourteen social workers to f**k off.
He told us to f**k off. But we didn't.
And we still haven't.'
Agency: Bartle Bogle Hegarty London
Art Director: Mark Reddy
Client: Barnardo's
Copywriter: Nick Gill
Creative Director: Nick Gill
Photographer: Kiran Master
Images reproduced with
kind permission of Kiran Master
c/o Burnham Niker, and Barnardo's

Simplicity and understatement

The well-worn piece of advice to 'keep it simple' was never more relevant than when applied to art direction. Simplicity in design and layout is more likely to make your advert visually compelling, attention grabbing, and easier to develop in terms of a visual hierarchy. In most cases, good art direction, as with good design, involves a process of stripping out rather than adding on; or to put it another way, of subtraction rather than addition.

It's not always what you choose to show, but instead what you choose not to show, that can define good art direction.

Subtraction

Once you have your idea visualised on paper or computer screen, try looking at what you can omit or subtract, either in terms of design elements, or in terms of the content of the image itself. Two ways of doing this that we've already looked at earlier in this chapter are to crop the image or to zoom-in close on some aspect or detail of the image. Look also at the elements that appear within the image. Is there anything that detracts from the key image or draws attention to itself at the cost of the advertising message? The image background may be important in terms of providing some kind of context for your image or simply locating it in terms of environment or setting; however, it can also be very distracting or add to the general 'busyness' of the advert.

If, for example, you are using an image of a cooked meal on a plate, served up on a table in a restaurant, how much information does the image need to communicate?

If the advertising message is presenting the ambience of the restaurant itself, it may be important to include a wider angle of view featuring the plate of food in the foreground and some aspect of the restaurant itself in the background.

If the emphasis of the advertising message is instead focused on the appeal of the food, then it may be a better idea to fill the image frame with a close-up shot of the food on the plate. You then have to decide just how close to zoom-in on the food – extreme close-up to allow the viewer to explore the almost abstract landscape that may be created, or zoom-out a little to include the edge of the full plate and part of the table, to present a more recognisable image with just enough visual cues for the viewer to establish the context. Another way to ensure that the visual emphasis is directed on the appropriate elements of the image is to use 'depth of field'.

By varying the aperture of the camera lens during a photo shoot, the photographer can change and control the depth of field in the resulting image, focusing selectively on individual objects or on a range of objects within the field of view. By adjusting the depth of field, emphasis can shift from one aspect of the image to another. It can help the art director in establishing the visual hierarchy of an image and direct the viewer to a focal point.

The well-worn adage, 'less is more', may seem to be a bit of a cliché, but it's a good idea to have this thought at the back of your mind whenever you are art directing advertising material.

Simplicity

The real beauty of a great idea can be its simplicity. When this is the case, that simplicity should be mirrored in the art direction. It's often tempting to keep adding further elements to the design of the advert, sometimes in an attempt to explain more about the product; at other times, to embellish or extend the cleverness of the idea. Without suitable restraint, it's easy to overwork the idea or to make it more complex than it needs to be. Some of the most memorable advertising campaigns have used understatement to great advantage. An advert can often have more impact when a simple, understated visual treatment unexpectedly leads your audience to a powerful thought or message.

Simplicity and understatement

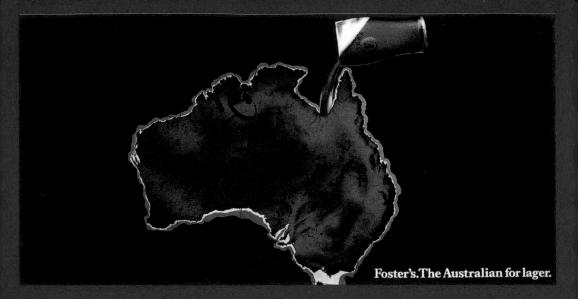

Foster's. The Australian for lager.

Above:
Keeping it simple
Take one map of Australia, a pint
of Foster's lager and a few strokes of
a marker pen to communicate the
brand proposition in a simple and
amusing fashion – that Foster's is
'The Australian for lager'.
Art Director: Warren Brown
Client: Foster's
Image courtesy of the
Advertising Archives

Right:
Using depth of field
In this advert for the VW Polo car,
the clever use of a shallow depth of
field provides the art director with an
opportunity to present the advertising
proposition in an entertaining and
witty fashion, finishing with the simple
copyline: 'Surprisingly ordinary prices'.
Agency: BMP DDB London
Client: Volkswagen Group
Creative Director: Jeremy Craigen
Photographer: Paul Reas

Polo L. £8,240 ⑦

Surprisingly ordinary prices ⑦

A way with words: Depth of field

The term 'depth of field' is used to describe a photographic effect where the range of objects that are in focus (from those that are nearest, to those that are furthest from the camera lens), increases or decreases as the lens aperture becomes smaller or larger, respectively.

The wider the aperture of the camera lens, the shallower the depth of field. So typically, with the camera lens opened to its widest aperture, everything behind and in front of the object you are focusing on will be out of focus to varying degrees, depending on how far from that object they are.

With the smallest aperture, the photographer can achieve a much greater depth of field, where the range of objects that are in focus increases, allowing sharp definition on foreground objects and objects in the distant background.

Simplicity and understatement

Which of these three kids is wearing Fisher Price anti-slip roller skates?

Recycle paper. Save trees. *GREENPEACE*

Left
The power of omission

Sometimes it's not so much a case of 'what you choose to show' as 'what you choose *not* to show' that can add drama and impact to the image. In this press advert for Fisher-Price anti-slip roller skates, we are drawn to the vacant space of the double-page spread and visualise in our mind's eye the other two 'kids' that the headline ('Which of these three kids is wearing Fisher Price anti-slip roller skates?') refers to, lying somewhere on the ground and out of camera view.
Image courtesy of the
Advertising Archives

Below left
The power of simplicity and understatement

The message: 'Recycle paper. Save trees,' is presented by laying a piece of white paper, torn from its spiral binding, over a green, grass-like background. An inspired creative insight where simplicity makes the effect more powerful, in this Greenpeace advert.
Agency: JWT Phillipines
Art Directors: Dave Ferrer, Joey Ong
Client: Greenpeace
Copywriters: Dave Ferrer, Joey Ong
Photographer: Francis Rivera

Give it a go

Take a look at the preceding image of the Greenpeace poster urging people to recycle paper. It's comprised simply of four elements: the sheet of paper, the grass-like background, the copyline and the logo.

Using the same four elements (no more, no less), find at least 20 different ways to art direct this poster. Use quick marker-pen layouts to experiment with different options with regard to the size, orientation and positioning of each element in relation to the other elements.

For example, you may zoom in on the perforations on the paper to show fewer 'trees', or not even a single one! You could change the colour of the paper, or position the copyline in the middle of the paper at a different size or in another typeface. You could change the position of the 'horizon'. The options are practically limitless and you should have no problems creating 20 different variations of the original ad. The real challenge is to see if you can find a better art-direction solution than the original one.

Creating a distinct look for the brand

Creating a distinct look for the brand is another important role of art direction. In the words of art director Ron Brown, it's all about 'origination', not 'imitation'. In a competitive market of similar, competing brands all offering similar benefits, identical standards of quality and performance, it's sometimes only the brand's identity that differentiates it from the competition. These days, it's quite rare to find a brand with a truly unique selling proposition (USP). In such cases, it's the advertising and other marketing media that have to create a perceived uniqueness for the brand. Ultimately, the look of the advertising should be unique to that brand in a manner that becomes distinctly associated with it at a glance.

Right
'Owning' a visual style
Some organisations and brands, such as *The Economist* magazine, have become associated with a certain visual style and content that is predominant throughout their advertising and overall marketing communication. The 'b#' advert (top left) alludes to the mental acuity or quick-wittedness of the magazine's projected readership (signalling them to 'be sharp'); while the other campaign ad (bottom right) plays on the fact that the name 'Jordan' is shared by both 'a Middle Eastern country with a 3.3% growth rate' and a British celebrity glamour model.
Agency: Abbott Mead Vickers BBDO
Client: *The Economist*
Creative Directors: Paul Belford, Nigel Roberts
Typographer: John Tisdall

The ingredients of house-style

The epic advertising campaigns for Benson & Hedges and Silk Cut, (mentioned on pages 60–65), created a distinct look that became inextricably linked to their respective brands. Sometimes it's a soundtrack, or the use of a well-known celebrity, or even the tone of voice expressed in the copywriting that may add to that distinctiveness; but in terms of art directing print-based adverts, it's the manner in which all of the visual elements combine together to create a look that becomes synonymous with the house-style of the brand.

b#

The Economist

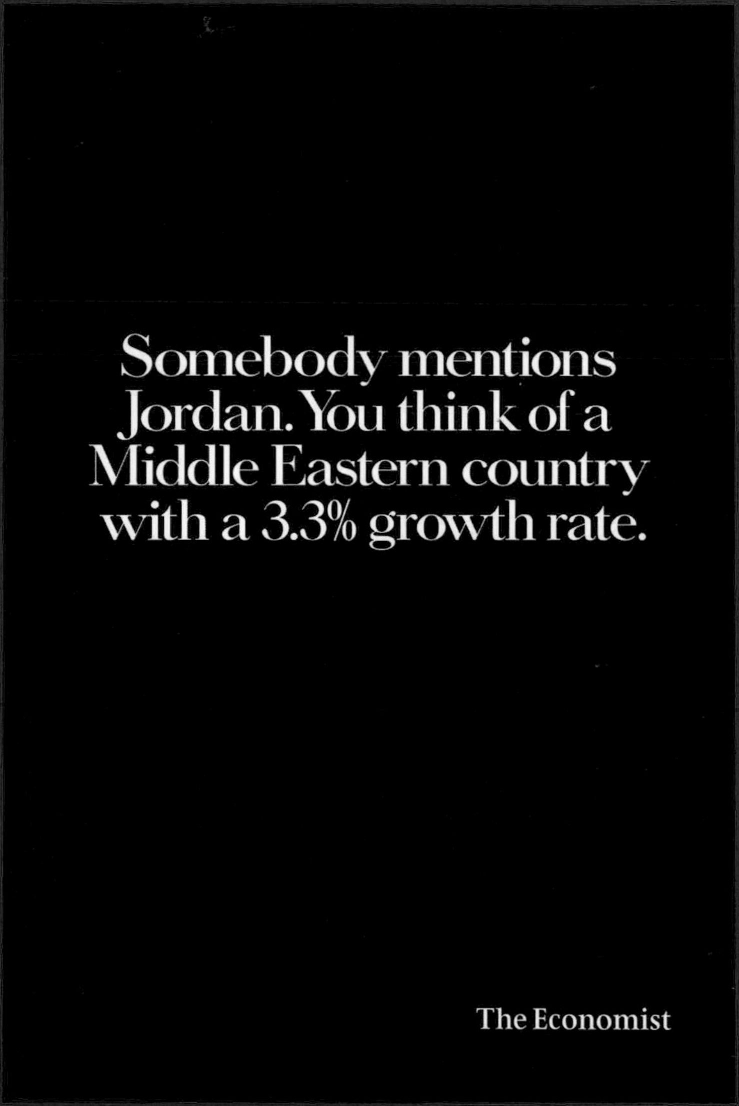

Somebody mentions Jordan. You think of a Middle Eastern country with a 3.3% growth rate.

The Economist

Creating a distinct look for the brand

To be.

The Economist

Shine and rise.

The Economist

Finding a 'look' that's right for the brand

In achieving a distinctive look, good art direction should remain sympathetic to the brand in terms of style and tone of voice. It should 'fit' with the character of the brand. That's not to say that it can't be original, surprising and unexpected. There's no reason why an advert for a car, a perfume, a supermarket or a can of beans needs to look like an advert for a car, a perfume, a supermarket or a can of beans. Each of those things are product categories, and the most distinctive brands tend to break free from the category stereotypes, sometimes redefining those stereotypes in the process.

Leading advertising creative Al Young once described the process of developing the 'look' of advertising as one that involves 'finding the right kind of wrongness'. In other words, discovering the one thing that doesn't fit comfortably with the generic tone and style of other products of the same genre, but that does still fit perfectly with the character of the brand itself, has appeal for the target audience and that elevates it from the rest of the competition. It's a fact that the most memorable moments in life are often those that are unexpected or on some occasions, simply provide a break from the normal routine. The same is true of advertising. Your audience will quickly forget adverts that look like every other advert for the same type of product and fit a generic template.

Sometimes the brand itself is 'mould-breaking' in its design or operation and deserves nothing less than an advertising campaign that reflects this.

A good example of this is the Apple Macintosh computer. In the 1980s, Apple revolutionised the computer market with the launch of the Macintosh computer. Innovative product design was mirrored by an equally innovative advertising campaign that made references to an Orwellian theme and announced that: 'On January 24th, Apple Computers will introduce Macintosh and you'll see why 1984 won't be like 1984.' The advertising looked nothing like the more conventional computer campaigns that people were used to seeing. Apple continue to create products today that challenge conventional boundaries in terms of both function and aesthetics. Similarly, their advertising maintains a fresh and innovative approach in its creative strategy and design.

Today, an increasing number of organisations and their agencies appear to understand the need to identify the essence of the brand itself (or a 'brand truth'), and reflect that in the tone of voice and general look of the advertising. This is an essential part of the branding process in which advertising plays a major role.

Creating a distinct look for the brand

iPod

Left
Creating a 'look' that reflects the essence of the brand
A unique and innovative style can become synonymous with the brand, particularly if that brand has a reputation for innovation itself. Apple's revolutionary approach to product design was echoed in their Orwellian-themed campaign to launch the Macintosh computer in 1984 (facing page, top left) and later on in their trendsetting campaign for the Apple iPod.

Apple Macintosh launch
Agency: Chiat/Day Inc. Advertising, LA
Art Director: Brent Thomas
Client: Apple Computer Inc.
Copywriter: Steve Hayden
Director: Ridley Scott
Production Company: RSA Films

Apple iPod
Agency: TBWA Worldwide, Inc.
Client: Apple Inc.
Photographer: Kai Regan

The process of creating the adverts involves a series of creative stages. At the outset, there is the task of generating the ideas themselves, sometimes referred to as ideation. Once the overall concept has been established and subsequent ideas formulated, then comes the task of art directing those ideas and writing the copy or script. At this stage, the art director will be involved in making a series of creative decisions that range from visual layout and style to the choice of medium (such as photography or illustration), and the selection of specialists to produce the final work.

Getting prepared

The creative process begins with the brief. Having a good understanding of the advertising message and who it's aimed at is vital to the success of any advertising concepts and although the brief should define the proposition and prospect (target audience) in explicit terms, it's up to you to dig deeper. In order to communicate with your target audience, it's important to have a thorough knowledge and understanding of their needs and desires and of how the brand can help them to fulfil these. It's equally important to get familiar with the product or brand.

The key to creativity is to ask lots of questions. The difficult bit is knowing which questions to ask. At the preparation stage, the most important questions to *answer* are: 'Who are you talking to?' and 'What do you want to say?' Only then can you go on to look at how you're going to say it.

Who are you talking to?

The brief may specify your target audience in terms of age, gender and socio-economic groups, but that does little to really 'bring them to life' when you have to visualise them as real people and not just as statistics. In order to communicate in a meaningful and convincing manner, you'll need to find out much more about the individuals that your advertising is aimed at. It's easy to make assumptions about your audience, or even worse, to simply stereotype them. If you do this, the chances are that you'll either get it completely wrong or, at best, simply fail to get their attention. If your audience can see that you understand exactly how they feel and what they want, they're more likely to listen to what you have to say.

In order to gain a deeper understanding of your audience, try pinpointing someone you personally know who fits the same profile. Have a checklist of questions that need to be answered in terms of their lifestyle, such as their taste in music, fashion, cars, sport, leisure, entertainment and literature. What hobbies and interests do they have? What films or television programmes do they enjoy? Which books, newspapers or magazines do they read? What are their likes or dislikes in general? What makes them happy, sad, angry, amused, anxious or excited? Do they have any strong opinions or feelings about the type of product you are advertising, or anything in general? What do they think about your specific client's brand?

What are you saying?

Although the brief will outline the advertising message or proposition, the way in which you interpret and present it is at the root of advertising ideation. For example, the brief may state that the advertising message should tell your audience that the brand of chocolate you're selling contains half the calories of other brands of chocolate. Your task is to find a more interesting way of communicating that message. In the previous chapter, we examined how it's important to look beyond the advertising proposition, to look at what this *really* means for the audience. In this instance, half the calories could mean 'half the guilt' or even 'twice the enjoyment'. It's then simply a case of finding an original, attention-grabbing way of expressing this.

Discovering unusual or interesting facts about the brand can be the key to success when you're trying to find a unique way of demonstrating the proposition. The best way to make these 'discoveries' is to talk to people who use, sell or make the brand. Find out if they've got any interesting stories to tell you, or whether they know any interesting things that they've discovered about the brand. It also helps to have some first-hand experience of the brand. Try using it yourself. If it's a physical object of some kind, then handle it, examine it, and take it apart if necessary. Find something that you can tell your target audience about the product that they didn't already know.

A way with words: Ideation

Ideation is the creative phase that involves the generation of ideas and concepts. It literally means 'idea creation', and so although it may not be the most widely used word to describe this, it's probably the most appropriate. More common terms such as brainstorming, mind-mapping or free-association are really, in fact, techniques and approaches that can lead to ideation.

From visuals to the finished work

Once the advertising concept and any campaign ideas have been approved, it's a case of experimenting with different layouts and art directing the visual material to achieve the best effect. At the end of Chapter 1, we looked at the process of using fast thumbnail sketches and 'one-stroke' marker visuals to explore alternative layouts and to make key decisions regarding the look of the adverts and the campaign in general. The advantage of marker-pen thumbnail sketches and scamps is that they're fast and enable you to quickly see what *is* going to work and what just isn't. It follows that the faster you can sketch your ideas out, the more ideas you'll be able to produce in the time you have available.

Using scamps and visuals to communicate the idea

Whilst quick scamps and marker-pen visuals can help you make some early decisions regarding the layout of the advert, they will also provide a means of communicating your ideas to others, such as photographers, illustrators, typographers, stylists and directors. For a start, there's the creative director who will need to be convinced that your idea is worth developing further. He or she will have to make a final decision on what creative work will be presented to the client. In most agencies, the creative director won't expect highly finished visuals at this stage, as most have the ability to see the potential in even the roughest of 'stick-men' sketches. However, before they can be presented to the actual client, they would normally need to be visualised to a higher standard of finish.

The level of finish required for the client presentation will depend largely on the client and their relationship with the agency. Whilst some clients may declare that they only want to see rough ideas, in reality, they often need to see something that's a closer approximation of how the finished advert may look. There is, of course, a danger that if you present something that's too highly finished, the client may forget that the visual isn't the final advert, and may become concerned with the lack of attention to detail and overall production quality. It's a case of getting the balance right and being aware that every client will have different expectations.

Below and right
Getting ideas down on paper
Preliminary visuals and scamps
allow different design layouts to be
explored and decisions to be made
over the final look of the campaign,
as illustrated by these scamps and
ensuing print ads for Barclays Bank.
Agency: EHS Brann
Art Director: Jamie Pulley
Client: Barclays Bank
Copywriter: Emma Braund

Photography

The choice of photography over illustration or simply a plain typographic image is normally determined very early on in the creative process. The development of digital photography, together with the proliferation of post-production tools and a host of computer software designed for retouching and manipulating images, makes the use of photography an attractive and flexible option. Although many photographers still use traditional film, the difference in the quality of digital images is hardly discernible in most advertising media. The benefits offered by digital photography in terms of speed, control and electronic transportability will, in most cases, far outweigh any concerns about the advantages of film grain over pixels.

The power of the photographic image

Photography can enable you to convey a wide range of moods and help to establish a 'tone of voice' for the campaign. Our frequent exposure to journalistic images in newspapers and magazines means that photography is often associated with factual material and it can consequently add credibility or an element of believability to your campaign. Although 'the camera never lies,' the selective cropping of the image, focus on detail, angle of view and the capacity of the still image to be removed from its original context all enable the art director to present the subject matter from an alternative perspective. Add to this the many post-production tools and techniques that are available, and you have the ability to change, distort and embellish the image in many different ways to add both power and drama to it, or to simply underline and reinforce the brand message.

In some cases, you may find that archive photos or news pictures can provide the perfect image for your advert.

Photography as a tool for reframing

In the previous chapter, we looked at how the ability to present visual material in fresh, novel and unexpected ways involved showing familiar things in unfamiliar ways, or making the usual, unusual and the ordinary, extraordinary. Well-considered and clever use of photography can enable this and at the same time create the high level of reframing that is evident in some of the most thought-provoking and impactful campaigns that we see. It begins with a creative insight or observation on the part of the creative team. It could simply be an observation that when you look at something from a certain angle or proximity, it looks like something else. By using photography to depict something in a different way, or by placing visual emphasis on it (or part of it), you can direct the viewer to see things that they hadn't noticed before and help them make personal 'discoveries' that will engage them with your advertising.

Custom photography or stock images?

A decision has to be made over whether to commission bespoke photography for the campaign or to instead use stock images from photo libraries or other archive sources. Whilst stock photography can provide a ready available reference source of images, those images can often compromise the original concept if they are not faithful to the visual idea that you had in mind. Another potential problem with stock photography is that the images that you choose to use may not be exclusively used by your brand and can sometimes have an 'overused' look and feel about them. Custom photography not only ensures exclusivity of use, it also provides an opportunity for the art director to make certain that the final image does not deviate from the initial idea. It further allows the art director and photographer a chance to experiment with variations of that image. Sometimes, opportunities to experiment with camera angles, the position of models, furniture and props and different facial expressions can present themselves during the shoot.

On the other hand, custom photography can be expensive, and if your client is advertising on a relatively small budget, appropriate stock images may be a more suitable resource. There was a time when stock photos tended to be fairly generic in terms of style and subject matter, and easily identifiable as 'ready-made' images. These days, stock photos tend to be wider-ranging in terms of themes, subjects, concepts and photographic styles.

Photography

Right and facing page
Manipulating the photographic image
In these adverts for children's charity Barnardo's, designed with the campaign message 'Giving children back their future', the availability of advanced post-production tools enables both subtle and dramatic manipulation of photographic images. Today, there is very little that the imagination can perceive or conjure that a photographic image cannot in turn depict.
Agency: Bartle, Bogle and Hegarty, London
Art Directors: Chris Felstead, Gary McNulty
Client: Barnardo's
Copywriters: Chris Felstead
Photographer: Peer Lindgreen
Images reproduced with kind permission of Peer Lindgreen, and Barnardo's

Below right
Using photography to make the ordinary, extraordinary
Photography can be used to present ordinary things in extraordinary ways. The Images created for this Haagen Dazs campaign are both ambiguous and engaging, as in this advert for their 'cookies and cream' ice cream.
Agency: Leo Burnett Connaghan & May, Melbourne
Art Director: Tone Walde
Client: Pillsbury Australia/ Haagen Dazs
Image courtesy of the Advertising Archives

Illustration

There will be occasions where the use of illustration may be more appropriate than photography. In some cases, it could be that the image naturally tends towards an illustrative treatment, and at other times it may be that the use of illustration is part of the overall creative idea. It's worth bearing in mind that some illustrative techniques also border on photography; similarly, some photographic images have an illustrative quality about them. Digital technology has enabled illustrators and photographers to push the boundaries of both disciplines, so that contemporary images are often a hybrid of both mediums.

When to use illustration

One of the most common uses of illustration in advertising can be seen in campaigns where the creative team are aiming to emulate a particular illustrative style. For example, it could be a pastiche of the technical style found in certain textbooks or instruction manuals, or the cartoon style found in comic magazines, or the type of illustrations found in children's storybooks.

In some cases, an illustration can convey a message that may be more difficult to communicate using a photographic image. It's often the case that the use of a pen, pencil, paintbrush or other illustrative medium can allow you to place a special emphasis on one aspect of the image that would be more difficult to convincingly manipulate photographically. In some ways, an illustration, as a personal interpretation of the subject matter, has greater 'artistic licence' to manipulate and distort reality, whereas photography is often expected to provide a more accurate visual representation.

There are occasionally ways in which you may wish to portray the brand that are only possible – or are at least more appropriate – through the use of illustrative techniques. It may be that the product or brand has to be depicted doing incredible things that, in reality, would be impossible for it to undertake. If photography were to be used in such a case, it may seem as though you were trying to fool your audience, whereas an illustration can sometimes be perceived as being less intrinsically deceptive.

Illustration

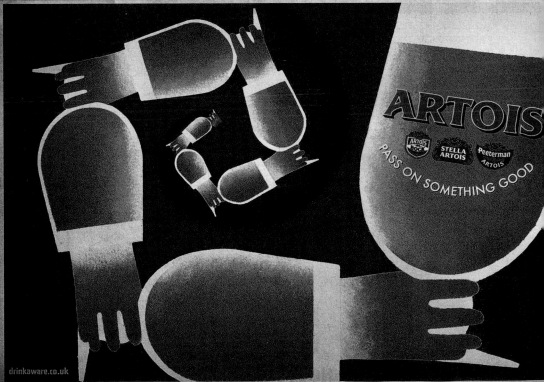

Left

Using illustration to create a retro look

Illustration is used to create a retro-style look for these Stella Artois adverts, which emphasise the brand's heritage, 'A brewing tradition for 30 generations'.

Agency: Lowe London
Brand: Artois
Client: InBev
Illustrator: David Lawrence
Typographers: Sebastien Delahaye, Dave Towers

Adopting a distinctive style of illustration for your advertising can help to establish a strong visual identity for the brand, as well as a high level of visual consistency and cohesiveness across all marketing communication associated with the brand. To this end, it's often worth considering illustrators who have a unique and distinctive style that hasn't yet been adopted or discovered by other brands, particularly those brands with which your brand is in direct competition.

Illustration

Right
Using the product as the illustrative medium
In this campaign for Marmite, the product itself is used to illustrate the other things that people tend to either love or hate, from hairy chests and sandals, to mullet hairstyles. Marmite's slogan, 'You either love it or hate it' has entered common parlance in the UK and become a popular way of describing things which tend to polarise public opinion.
Agency: DDB
Art Director: Damien Bellon
Client: Unilever Bestfoods
Copywriter: Thierry Albert
Creative Director: Jeremy Graigen
Illustrator: Dermot Flynn
Photographer: Andy Rudak

Look for opportunities where illustration can help communicate an aspect of the product or service, in a way that photography can't.

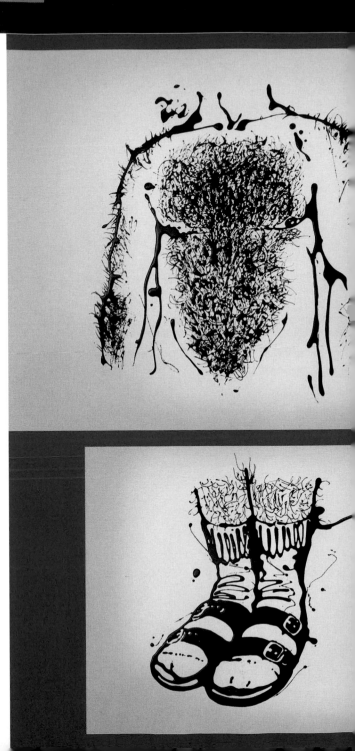

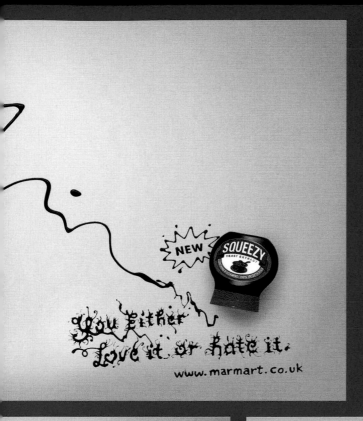

Typography

The choice of typeface for headlines, straplines, slogans, body copy and any other occasion where words appear in print is an opportunity to give those words visual expression. Every typeface has a personality of its own which, with creative insight, can enhance the advertising message by emphasising a tone of voice, an attitude, a mood, a visual style, or the overall theme of the campaign itself. Using typography to strengthen the advertising message in this way requires a good understanding of how visible language can conjure different feelings and emotions across your target audience.

Using type to enhance the advertising message

Typography is a specialist field in its own right and, in most cases, where it's a major feature of the advert, a typographer would normally be hired to craft the type in order to achieve the effect that the art director desires to create. However, as an art director, it's well worth becoming aware of a few basic guidelines and principles for yourself, along with a general understanding of how typography can add an extra dimension to your art direction.

There are many different variables that can determine how a certain typeface can affect audience perception. Most typefaces can be broadly categorised into one of three types: serif, sans serif and script faces. Each of these has its own distinctive personality and each can express different moods and meanings depending on the context in which it is used; its size, colour, juxtaposition and relationship to other elements within the advert, not to mention what the copy itself reads. Visual differences between one typeface and another similar one may seem negligible at a glance, but when the type is set as a headline, or in columns of text, the difference in appearance and emotional quality can range from subtle to extreme.

Typography can make the need for an image redundant. A powerful headline, crafted in a manner that is synonymous with the brand message, can be all that is needed. Typography can also become the image itself. Examples range from the more conventional 'headline only' solutions, to something more elaborate where multiple or single words are crafted to depict an image.

Typography essentially constitutes the marriage of verbal and visual communication and it can have a major impact on the 'tone of voice' of a campaign. Good typography in advertising doesn't exist merely to draw attention to itself. It's ultimately there to facilitate communication of the advertising message and should not distract the audience from receiving that message.

Type can shout or it can whisper. It can be light-hearted or deadly serious. It can express authority or anarchy. It can denote corporate affiliation or independence. It can help convey a cool, contemporary image for your brand or demonstrate a stake in older, traditional values. Sometimes, the art director may be limited by corporate guidelines regarding the choice of typeface and its various manifestations within an advertising campaign. These are often fixed, mandatory guidelines given in the creative brief; however, whenever you have the chance – experiment!

As an art director, the best way to develop a sensitivity to typography is to study other great examples of print-based advertising that use typography well. Ask yourself: why does it work so well and how does it work?

A way with words: Lorem ipsum

Lorem ipsum is a standard piece of Latin-based text that is often 'cut and pasted' into advertising visuals and comps to simulate the appearance of body copy on a page as it approximates the distribution of words that are typeset in English text. The most common form of *Lorem ipsum* text reads as follows: 'Lorem ipsum dolor sit amet, consectetur adipisicing elit, sed do eiusmod tempor incididunt ut labore et dolore magna aliqua. Ut enim ad minim veniam, quis nostrud exercitation ullamco laboris nisi ut aliquip ex ea commodo consequat. Duis aute irure dolor in reprehenderit in voluptate velit esse cillum dolore eu fugiat nulla pariatur. Excepteur sint occaecat cupidatat non proident, sunt in culpa qui officia deserunt mollit anim id est laborum.'

Typography

JFK, LAX, ORD, MIA, RDU, BOS, DFW. EVERY DAY, PDQ.

Most people tend not to speak in code, so to translate, that's New York, Los Angeles, Chicago, Miami, Raleigh/Durham, Boston and Dallas/Fort Worth. But it really doesn't matter what the IATA, sorry, the International Air Transport Association calls them, does it? It's the fact that you have to get there that's important. And because none of these cities is less than three thousand miles from London, you'll probably want the airline that takes you there to provide the highest standards of comfort and service possible. In that case you'll be pleased to hear that American Airlines flies to all of them, non-stop from London, every day. As you might expect, being American ourselves we're very proud of the reputation Americans have for their level of service and hospitality, and nowhere will you find this reputation more deserved than on an American Airlines flight. We think we have a good idea what you want from an airline and our aim is simple; to provide the most comfortable, relaxing, stress-free environment you're ever likely to experience on board an aircraft. We have a highly experienced and attentive cabin crew, a varied selection of wines, a team of nationally acclaimed chefs designing innovative, mouth-watering menus, and we offer great in-flight entertainment. So, if you're looking for a little TLC on your way to the US, try AA, OK?

American Airlines offers over twenty daily non-stop flights from the UK to the seven US gateway cities in our headline. From these we can easily connect you to hundreds more throughout the US, Canada, Latin America and the Caribbean. Visit americanairlines.co.uk for details.

We know why you fly™
AmericanAirlines

Left
Using typography to emulate or reflect the imagery
In this campaign for American Airlines, the body copy is typeset in a style that emulates an American city skyline. The bold upper case, sans serif font that is used for the headline echoes this theme, by the way in which the words are stacked high upon each other and sit vertically flush to define the left-hand edge of the advert.
Agency: McCann Erickson
Client: American Airlines
Copywriters: Robert Campbell, Dean Webb
Photographer: Nick Meek
Typographer: Gary Todd

Typography

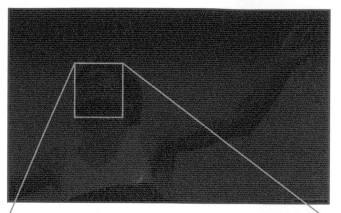

Mind you this could be my big break If that girl can get on TV for
legs go! Bloody hell – not another hill Aren't there any that go d
re This is awful And to think I wanted to join the SAS Well at least
:bab with chilli sauce and bugger the consequences And a large
ons? What wouldn't I give to make this pain go away now? I'm g
ng themselves while I'm suffering I need a new set of mates I'll
p into that church and pray for a new set of legs Preferably the v
me and send him some hate mail Do the League Against Cruel S
I downhill from here I'm referring to my life not the race unfortun
1g to drive everywhere in future Woe is me It'll be Whoa is me If
It leg is longer than the right one now I can't stop my head from
carpet? I'm going to write to my MP about it I want questions
every step I take These wrap around reflective shades that the t
f way OK, think positive – there's plenty of room for improvement
's ago? I think I've aged ten years in the last two hours Isn't exa
ver been so envious of someone on a stretcher I need some so
alf marathon Next year I'll do a fun run instead, if there is such a
his palaver Why don't they have half-time? Ho ho ho, Santa's jus
1e energy for the last three yards I can't believe I could be in a p
ull me along It was better when I was running in amongst the old
rget all the pain I think I'm beyond feeling any further pain Are
eating anymore I'm having a coronary This stitch isn't going Tha
gotten how to run Shall I walk for a bit? I would do deep breaths
Knew I should have gone to church Give me that wheelchair Wha
st Why 26.2 miles, it's not even a round number? Is that my car
1ome I wonder if everyone feels this bad? How can they do this

Left

Using typographic images
Sometimes the typography can
be inseparable from the image.
The image of the athlete (former UK
athlete and Olympic gold medallist,
Sebastian Coe) in the Adidas advert
shown here is comprised of lines of
text which capture the thoughts of the
long-distance runner. Each word is
printed at different weights and tones
to make up the image in a mosaic,
pixel-like fashion, as shown in this
detail (bottom left).
Agency: TBWA/London
Client: Adidas
Copywriters: Paul Silburn,
Stuart Harkness, Kerry Gooden
Creative Directors: Trevor Beattie,
Paul Silburn
Photographer: Keystone/Stringer
Typographer: Dan Beckett
Image courtesy of Getty Images

Give it a go

Experiment with different type forms and styles with some of your own print-based concepts. Start by shortlisting about six different typefaces. Choose some that seem appropriate and some that don't – you may be surprised! Start with the headline. Using a computer, set each of your selected typefaces at a variety of sizes. This will give you a good idea of the look and 'feel' of the typeface when it's actually set as a line of copy. If the headline is likely to run to more than a single line, then try several variations with each line set flush left, flush right, centred and justified. Alternatively, you may also want to consider running the headline around another visual element within the advert, or even setting it at a jaunty angle across the image.

There are a countless number of other options that you can experiment with, ranging from the colour or opacity of the typeface, to the depth of the line spacing and selective emphasis on words through variation in size, weight or style. Above all, consider the relationship of the headline to the central image (if there is one).

A good rule of thumb to rely on is that visual contrast normally works well. So if you have a bold or dramatic image, consider a small, understated piece of typesetting for the headline. Conversely, if you want the headline to be set in a bold, dramatic manner, then consider a smaller, 'quieter' image. In other words, don't let the headline and the image compete against each other.

Once you've crafted the look of the headline, you should consider the appearance of the body copy in a similar manner. Visually, this is likely to appear as blocks of 'grey' text. You can simulate this by using *Lorem ipsum* text, which can be cut and pasted in any typeface, size, weight or other format you require. Once again be experimental: try different column sizes and shapes. Break them up and move them around the page. Try something unusual and don't be satisfied with the most obvious or conventional layout. You can physically print out blocks of *Lorem ipsum* text, cut them up with scissors and rearrange them by hand if you find this easier or faster than working on a computer screen. Remember that your body copy doesn't have to be the same typeface as your headline and that once again, contrast can often prove to be more effective.

Planning and storyboarding commercials

A storyboard provides a visual medium for mapping out the various scenes, flow of action and general direction of a commercial from start to finish. As well as a means of presenting your idea to the creative director, account team and client, it allows you to brief all of the other parties involved in the production of the commercial. At the outset, however, it is a means of planning the action and general storyline. When all of the scenes in your commercial have been developed and finalised, they will be drawn up fully on the storyboard as a series of around six to twelve frames for an average television commercial. This will normally be accompanied by a full script and direction notes on a separate piece of paper.

Right
Let the action tell the story
Sometimes, a short sentence at the end of a commercial – or perhaps even a slogan – is enough to explain or reframe the preceding visual action in a powerful and memorable way, as with the slogan '100% adrenaline' used in the final storyboard frame pictured here.
Image: Nik Mahon

Keep the story simple

Some would claim that the best ideas are the simplest ones. I know of at least one creative director at a major London agency who refused to look at any storyboard ideas unless the creative team involved could first present it to him in just four images or key frames. Bearing in mind that one of these key frames would include the opening image and another the closing image (with typically a slogan and voiceover), this only left two frames to describe the action in-between! Whilst I wouldn't recommend slavishly following this 'rule', it's a good discipline to try and simplify the action to a minimum number of frames when first planning your idea.
You can always add further frames when you come to produce the full storyboard, but this isn't normally necessary in the initial stages.

OPEN ON HELICOPTER FLYING OVER TOWER BRIDGE

CUT TO CAR DRIVING ACROSS BRIDGE BEING PURSUED BY HELICOPTER

CUT TO CLOSE-UP OF HELICOPTER

ZOOM OUT TO SHOW HELICOPTER AS SEEN FROM INSIDE CAR

CUT TO CLOSE-UP OF DRIVER'S FACE AS SHE WEAVES THROUGH OBSTACLES

100% ADRENALINE

CUT TO STILL SHOT OF CAR & SUPER: "100 % ADRENALINE"

Get the timing right

Be aware of the timing and duration of the commercial too. There's very little you can communicate in 30 seconds, or even in a full minute – so you have to keep the message simple. Television and cinema are powerful – but fleeting – mediums. If your audience missed something, there's no opportunity for them to scan over it again as they would probably do with a print advert. Don't overestimate how much action or script you can fit into the time you have. Remember that any form of dialogue or voiceover includes natural breaks and pauses between words and sentences. You'll also need to allow for a few seconds of 'lead-in' time at the beginning of the commercial, as well as some time at the end, before and after any words are spoken.

Make audio and visual work together

With very little time for a lengthy script in your commercial, the visual action has to work extra hard to communicate the advertising message. If a picture can say a thousand words, imagine the potential of the moving image when the audience are viewing 24 pictures (or frames) every second of your commercial. Don't, however, fall into the trap of trying to demonstrate every product benefit imaginable. Concentrate instead on simplicity and focus on a single message. As with the headline and image of a print advert, the script and images of a commercial have to complement each other in a way that enables one of these elements to give meaning to the other.

4

The choice of media is normally predetermined within the parameters of the creative brief. However, if opportunities to enhance the idea emerge through the use of alternative media, then the art director and copywriter will often explore these also.

As media channels diversify and consumers generally find themselves bombarded by advertising everywhere they turn, there is a need for individual advertisers to cut through the 'noise' and stand out from the rest of the competition with a focused, believable proposition that offers a clear benefit to the consumer. In order to achieve this, the creative team sometimes has to find fresh, unexpected and unconventional ways of using conventional media channels – or alternatively, find new, unconventional media.

Posters

Art directors love posters because they draw upon all of their skills to communicate a message in a single, memorable graphic image. It's a highly visible outdoor media that's difficult to ignore or filter out. While it's relatively easy to surf TV commercials or flip past magazine ads, it's not so easy to avoid the advertising message when confronted by it on a large-scale, strategically placed poster designed to capture your attention. New digital technology presents advertising creatives with an even broader toolbox of 'tricks', from moving images to interactive graphics. As part of a multimedia campaign approach, posters can also enable the advertiser to extend the effect of expensive TV campaigns by restating or further developing the themes introduced in commercials, thereby prompting recall of them.

Making the most of the location

One of the most important considerations when designing for outdoor media is the placement of the advert. Its location and immediate environment can have a significant bearing on the context of the message itself. Whilst the agency's media buyer may be prioritising location in terms of the target audience, and what percentage of that audience are likely to see the poster, the creative team (and the more creative media buyers) will look for other opportunities that a particular site may offer, and will question how the location itself could potentially become part of the advertising concept. As an art director, you may be able to find a creative solution that can be easily adapted or modified to suit a variety of different environments or environmental backdrops. On rare occasions, you may also be in a position to create a one-off idea for a single, prominent site that will attract a lot of your viewing audience and get people talking – or generate a real buzz!

Right
The world's first shadow poster
This advert inviting people to test drive the new Volkswagen Eos convertible was the world's first shadow poster. It projected the message ('Perfect weather for a test drive') on the ground below each time that the sun shone through – a good idea for a car that allows both driver and passengers the chance to make the most of sunny weather.
Agency: DDB Germany/Düsseldorf
Client: Volkswagen

Below
Making the image fit the location
This campaign for Amnesty
International was comprised of
200 posters, which were placed
in and around Switzerland to raise
awareness of and fuel debate on the
issue of human rights. Each poster
was individually created to match its
location and immediate surroundings,
to create a trompe l'œil effect and
present the action portrayed as
occurring in real time. Only the poster
headline revealed the 'trick' involved:
'It's not happening here. But it is
happening now.'
Agency: Walker
Client: Amnesty International
Creative Director: Pius Walker
Photographer: Federico Naef

Posters

Above and right
Blowing up the image –
quite literally!
Engineered to self-destruct exactly
on time, this enhanced poster was
designed to raise the profile of
Deadline Couriers in Auckland, and
their brand promise to deliver on
schedule. Stunts like this generate
media publicity beyond the
advertising itself.
Agency: Colenso BBDO
Art Directors: Jamis Hitchcock,
Josh Lancaster
Client: Deadline Express Couriers
Creative Director: Richard Maddocks
Production Company:
Rollercoaster Design

Making the most of the media

Generally speaking, posters can range from noticeboard to billboard size and larger. The key thing is to think big, and as always, keep it simple. It's amazing how the most mundane, everyday object can look spectacular when blown-up in size to fit a 48- or 96-sheet poster.

● ● ●

A poster idea should be kept simple. This also extends to the use of visual elements. In general, it's best to restrict yourself to just an image, a headline, a logo (or packshot) and a slogan – and in some cases you won't need all of these. One thing you certainly shouldn't incorporate is a large volume of body copy unless you can really guarantee that your audience will be compelled to stop and read it. This is rarely the case unless, in the case of cross-track posters (posters situated across the other side of a rail line from the passenger platform) for example, you have a captive audience.

The opportunity to show something larger than life can also force your audience to look more closely at a particular image and perhaps enable them to make a personal discovery in seeing something that they had not noticed before. Providing a visual solution that prompts thought, personal insights and a fresh perspective on a brand or an issue, is a fundamental goal in the creation of outstanding art direction. Sometimes, the interest will be in the detail, and the nature of this large-scale medium will enable you to focus in on such detail and create images that are visually compelling.

Outdoor media such as posters also present a good opportunity for you to generate free publicity. If your great idea is unusual, newsworthy or controversial enough to become a talking point, then other public media such as news programmes and the press may feature the campaign and extend its impact beyond the advertising media alone.

Make sure that there's also a good level of visual consistency across your entire poster campaign, extending to typography, type of imagery, use of photography or illustration, straplines and the general layout and style of the advert. This visual consistency should ideally be present across all media. That way your audience will come to recognise the advertising immediately, which in turn will enhance visibility, memorability and recall.

Magazine and press

When it comes to visibility, it could be argued that magazine and press adverts have a more difficult task than other print-based media. Audiences aren't generally interested in the adverts, they're interested in all the other material that their magazine contains: feature articles, current affairs, gossip, correspondence pages, stories, entertainment and possibly the classified adverts or recruitment pages if there's something specific that they're looking for. They tend to skip over the pages containing adverts and in order to get them to read yours, you first have to grab their attention amidst a sea of competing adverts and other textual material.

Getting noticed

A sure way to *prevent* your advert from getting noticed is to make it blend in with the rest of the magazine. It's well worth taking a look at the kind of publications that your advertising campaign will be appearing in to get a sense of visual style and readership. As the reader turns the pages of the magazine, he or she is more likely to stop at a page that looks different from the rest, and which to some extent may even look slightly out of place within the design framework of that magazine. It's all about surprising your audience and doing something unexpected. At this stage, it's worth revisiting some of the principles highlighted in Chapter 2 of this book, where we looked at the use of compelling images and unusual layout to create visual impact. In that same chapter, the importance of simplicity and understatement was also discussed. The combination of a compelling image and a simple, uncluttered layout is a winning combination that should make your advert stand out from the generally 'busy' appearance of the average magazine.

Be aware of the format of your advert and of its placing within the magazine. Does the size and shape of your advert present any creative opportunities and can you use its position in the magazine to garner some advantage in terms of the relationship between the advert and the surrounding magazine content?

Opportunities that magazines and the press offer

Magazine and press ads provide you with several opportunities that posters may not. For a start, the use of body copy to provide more information is something that's more viable in magazine adverts (although it's important that your audience don't have to read the body copy to understand the general idea). There's also the chance to focus more closely on specific groups or sections of your target audience through the selection of particular publications. You can even adapt the content of the advertisement and the phrasing of any copy to relate to the readership of a given magazine.

The use of a vocabulary that's exclusive to a particular section of your audience will demonstrate a certain level of knowledge and understanding of your audience that, in turn, will help to establish a greater level of confidence and trust in the brand. Just be careful that you're not trying to present the brand as too many different things to too many different people. It's still important to make certain that the tone of voice remains true to the brand.

There is also the physical medium of the magazine itself. Ask yourself: 'Is there anything else I can do to create more impact when the reader opens the page on which my advert is printed?' Does something fall out of the page? Does it trigger the playback of a digital sound recording? Is there something I can do with the page itself, such as tearing it, folding it, staining it, or using a different paper stock? Have bold creative ideas with regard to the use of the medium in this way, but make certain that the final idea is relevant to the brand proposition itself. There's no point in having an unusually novel and quirky idea unless it helps to demonstrate or underline the advertising message.

Magazine and press

Left and right
**Avoiding 'same-old-shots' and
visual clichés**
This magazine advert for Natan
Jewellery avoids the visual cliché
of close-up photographs depicting
gold watches and diamond-encrusted
jewellery in favour of a more
unconventional, 'intellectual' and
amusing approach to promoting
the brand.
Agency: F/Nazca Saatchi & Saatchi
Art Director: Sidney Araujo
Client: Natan Jewellery
Creative Directors: Fabio Fernandes,
Eduardo Lima
Photographer: Fabio Bataglia

**Grab attention by
surprising your audience.
First, work out what they
expect to see: then do
something different. For
example, it could be that
your audience expect to
see the product featured
in the advert. Instead of
showing the product, find
an unusual or dramatic way
to show its effect or benefit.**

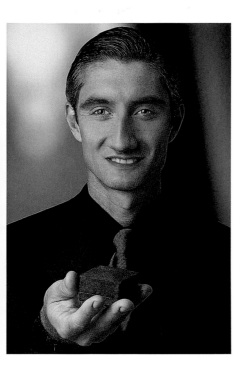

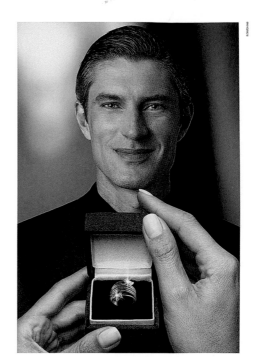

NataN
JOALHERIA O poder dos quilates.

Television and cinema

Television and cinema are both powerful visual media that use moving images and sound to captivate and motivate audiences. The moving image provides you with more scope to engage the audience and keep them guessing as to what may or may not be happening in the commercial. As the storyline unfolds, there are opportunities to confound the expectations of your audience up to the point where the advertising message is revealed in an unexpected 'twist'. By keeping your audience guessing, you engage them in a way that is similar to how TV soaps keep their audiences metaphorically 'glued' to the box. The human tendency to try to second guess what's going to happen next can be utilised by the art director to their advantage when planning out the commercial, and storyboarding the sequence of scenes and camera shots.

Don't talk too much!

Just as the process of art directing a print advert involves the use of images and typography in a complementary but impactful manner, television and cinema commercials require an equally sympathetic relationship between the moving images and the spoken word. As a general rule of thumb, don't employ too many words (spoken or typographic) if there's a lot of visual action going on in the commercial. Conversely, limit the amount of visual action if there's a lot to say. It could be the case that you have to present a lot of verbal or textual information, in which case it's best not to present a complex or busy visual scenario.

On the whole though, visual imagery has the potential to communicate more information in a faster and more memorable way. In some of the most effective commercials, the imagery is supported by just a short voiceover at the end. This can add meaning to the scene in a powerful and often thought-provoking or entertaining fashion. Sometimes you can say a lot more by speaking a lot less!

Right:
Telling a story to capture the audience's imagination
This commercial follows a man dressed in racing overalls as he embarks on an amazing journey, travelling in and on a series of landmark Honda vehicles, beginning with a humble moped and ending in a hot-air balloon. Throughout this time he mimes to the Andy Williams song *The Impossible Dream*. As the song reaches its climax and the balloon soars skyward from the foot of a waterfall a male voiceover concludes: 'I couldn't have put it better myself.'
Agency: Wieden+Kennedy
Art Director: Chris Groom
Client: Honda
Copywriter: Sean Thompson
Creative Directors: Tony Davidson, Kim Papworth

Online

Given our dependence on the internet in our everyday lives, it's no wonder that online advertising has become an increasingly attractive medium for advertisers. In an age where consumers expect to be able to interact with their favourite brands and engage with them on a personal level, online advertising offers advertisers a chance to initiate, cultivate and develop closer relationships with their audiences. There is arguably no other communication media where advertising creativity and marketing strategy are so closely interlinked, and the online creative needs to foster an awareness of the unique opportunities that the various forms of online advertising can offer.

Art directing online material

Online advertising embraces a broad panoply of communication platforms that include display advertising, virals, video, microsites, social media, mobile and in-game advertising. In terms of art direction, the fundamental need to have a creative idea and craft the look of the advertising so that it is visually compelling, memorable, stand-out and communicates the message in a clear and effective manner, remains the same as with any other advertising medium. The big difference for the art director is that he or she will need to think ahead in terms of functionality, as well as to anticipate the interface with the user at the other end. Simplicity is one of the primary considerations to bear in mind here, and planning out how the user will navigate through the pages of a microsite is one such example of this.

It is also important that you consider the limitations of the hardware. Pixelation and the colour range and quality of the computer screen need to be taken into account. Small images may lack clarity, and detail will then generally be lost, as will the definition of fine lines and fine typography when displayed at a relatively small point size. You should also be aware that the more complex the animations and layers that you build into your online material are, the greater the risk that it may run too slowly on the user's computer or just not work altogether. Don't assume that your audience all have the latest state-of-the-art, turbo-charged computers at their disposal.

A CHEQUE BOUNCED

IT RAINED

FIGHT

DOMESTIC

VIOLENCE

Agency: Saatchi & Saatchi NZ
Cinematographer: Nick Hutchinson
Client: Women's Refuge
Creative Director: Mike O'Sullivan
Designer: Musonda Katongo
Director: Nathan Price

Above
**Exploiting the interactive
potential of online media**
This interactive viral microsite
created for Women's Refuge was
designed to raise awareness about
the psychological damage caused
by verbal abuse, urging viewers to
'fight domestic violence'. It depicted
a woman's face that became bruised
or cut as the internet user yelled
into the computer's microphone.
As the yelling ceased, the injuries
would disappear.

Direct

Direct advertising is distinguished from other forms of advertising by the manner in which it sets out to communicate and engage more directly with the target audience, through a variety of different media such as direct mail, telemarketing, email and a range of online formats. Although recipients are targeted through the use of sophisticated databases, direct advertising material is usually unsolicited; therefore, if it's not well considered and designed, it runs the risk of being ignored, or worse still, annoying the recipient – as in the case of junk mail. More distinctively, direct advertising will incorporate a 'call to action' that requires a direct response from the recipient.

Art directing direct advertising

Direct advertising material is normally just one component of a much bigger integrated campaign. It's therefore important for the art director to have a broad view of how the direct advertising will integrate with the rest of the campaign, both in terms of concept and appearance. Art direction itself will typically be focused on graphic media such as online material, press ads and direct mail.

As direct advertising is often concerned with developing a lasting relationship with the recipients, there should be a sense of continuity flowing through the design and layout of these adverts. Both the art direction and the overall design of the advert should have a sense of 'one-to-one' communication embedded within them. You'll need to work closely with your copywriter to achieve this.

Right
'Rescue the vegetables' –
Promoting a direct response!
This integrated direct response campaign identified the fact that every single day in the UK, food is thrown away and wasted. The call to action – 'Your country veg needs YOU!' – urged the audience to rescue unwanted vegetables by adding Knorr Stock cubes to the cooking ingredients. The campaign humorously mimicked the format of political campaign posters and followed the traditional pre-Christmas media scheduling normally used by charity campaigns.
Agency: JWT London
Client: Unilever

A way with words: Call to action

Literally interpreted, the term 'call to action' is a statement that summons the consumer to act. It normally urges immediate action and in its most basic form uses common terms such as 'call now', 'write now' or 'click here'. It refers to the means by which you motivate your audience to take the next step and respond to your advert. Above all, the call to action has to be compelling enough to elicit the desired response. In other words, you have to give the recipient a good reason to respond. This reason could be something as simple as a limited offer, a special discount, or any other incentive that moves them emotionally to take instant action.

Ambient

Ambient advertising is defined by a number of distinctive characteristics. First and foremost, the location or setting in which the advert is placed is normally a key component of the advertising idea itself. Secondly, an ambient advert doesn't usually look or 'feel' like an advert – at least not at the outset. It often involves an unconventional use of familiar public space, surroundings and objects as part of the advertising media itself. Thirdly, ambient advertising is designed to take us unawares. The advertising is placed where we, as consumers, would least expect to find it. This enables it to slip under the 'radar' that normally enables us to filter out unsolicited marketing communication. By the time we realise it's an ad, we're already aware of the advertising message. So, in effect, it's advertising by stealth.

Generating a 'buzz'

Like other forms of advertising, it can be witty or deadly serious; but it should always be unexpected, emerging from the ambience of our surroundings. One final characteristic of a brilliant piece of ambient advertising is the buzz that it generates. It should get people talking – and excitedly telling their friends, relatives and colleagues about it. It may even prompt people to send photos from their mobile phones and so generate further publicity through other media channels. In this sense, it should have a 'viral' quality about it.

Right
Taking the audience by surprise
This park bench in Germany looks no different from the others – that is, until someone attempts to sit on it, causing it to deform. The small plate on the backrest reads: 'High time for Kellogg's Special K – 99% fat free,' highlighting the potential health benefits of eating this particular brand of Kellogg's breakfast cereal.
Agency: Leo Burnett
Art Director:
Alexander Michaelopoulos
Client: Kellogg Company
Copywriter: Anne Hampel
Creative Directors: Andreas Heinzel, Peter Steger
Photographer: Peter Steger

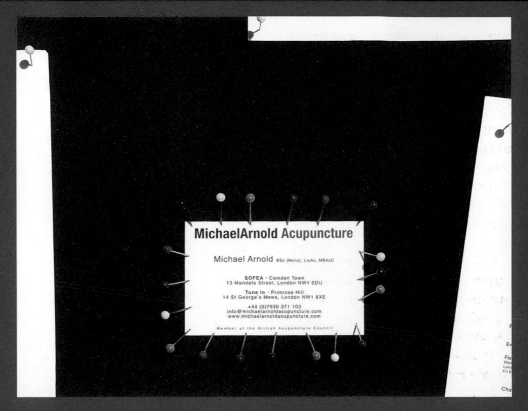

MichaelArnold Acupuncture

Michael Arnold BSc (Hons), LicAc, MBAcC

SOFEA · Camden Town
13 Mandela Street, London NW1 0DU

Tune In · Primrose Hill
14 St George's Mews, London NW1 8XE

+44 (0)7930 371 103
info@michaelarnoldacupuncture.com
www.michaelarnoldacupuncture.com

Member of the British Acupuncture Council

Höchste Zeit für
99% fettfrei.

Above
Using location in a witty way
Acupuncturist Michael Arnold
targeted local businesses with
the message that: 'acupuncture
can help cut staff absenteeism
caused by work-related stress.'
His advertising agency, Harrison
Troughton Wunderman, contacted
the Human Resources departments
of 20 companies where staff
were known to work long hours,
and arranged to have his card
pinned up on their noticeboards
in a very distinctive, yet highly
relevant, fashion.
Photo reproduced with
kind permission of Michael Arnold

Ambient

As well as air conditioning, the Polo Twist comes with alloy wheels, metallic paint, ABS, front electric windows and power steering, all as standard. Cool. For details of your nearest participating Volkswagen retailer, call 0800 333 666 or visit www.volkswagen.co.uk

Air conditioning as standard. Polo Tv

All prices referred to are rrp. Pearl effect is also available as standard. Official fuel consumption in mpg (litres/100km) the Polo range: urban 49.6 (5.7) – 27.2 (10.4); extra urban 68.9 (4.1) – 47.1 (6.0); combined 61.4 (4.6)

Above and right
Making the most of your ambient stunt

A life-size ice sculpture of the new VW Polo Twist was parked on a busy London street to promote the air conditioning that came 'as standard' with this model of car (right).

A photo of this sculpture was then used in a print campaign (above) and an ice cube tray that made Polo-shaped cubes was sent out as a direct mail piece.
Agency: DDB London, UK
Client: Volkswagen

Recognising ambient opportunities

The role of the art director may be less traditional when using ambient media; however, art directors do still need to create a visual impact with any campaign that relies on it. This can involve anything from visual puns to elaborate pastiche.

While print advertising allows the art director to show familiar things in unfamiliar ways, ambient advertising enables the art director to go a stage further and take familiar settings, architectural features, and commonplace items that we are confronted with every day, *and do something novel and unexpected with them*. The capacity to recognise ambient media opportunities in such locations and settings requires imagination, vision and, more often than not, a sense of drama. These are all qualities that a good art director should possess.

Although good ambient ideas can stand alone, they normally support a broader multimedia campaign. The important thing is to make sure that the key proposition is clearly communicated by the ambient idea. That way, it will reinforce the message that is being presented throughout the rest of the advertising.

Other media

In addition to the different media already outlined in this chapter, there are a variety of other media that the creative team may be involved in utilising as part of a broader campaign. The proliferation of new communication channels and the opportunities that digital technology and social networking offer now provide a rich choice when advertisers are formulating their marketing strategy. Whilst print-based images are always likely to have appeal, the familiar landscape of outdoor advertising is rapidly changing. The static images we are accustomed to seeing on poster sites and the sides of vehicles are gradually being replaced by animated digital images, challenging the traditional concept of art direction and pushing it into new dimensions.

Right
The 'evolution' of a viral campaign
This compelling piece of time-lapse film entitled 'Evolution' was produced to promote the Dove self-esteem workshops in Canada. It revealed the many camera, lighting, retouching, image-manipulation, make-up and hairdressing tricks that are involved in transforming an 'ordinary-looking' young woman into a stunningly beautiful billboard model. At the end of her amazing transformation, a voiceover comments: 'No wonder our perception of beauty is distorted.' When the 75-second viral film was uploaded to YouTube at no cost, it generated over 1.7 million views and, according to the blog-tracking service Technorati, became one of the top 15 most-linked-to videos amongst bloggers.
Agency: Ogilvy & Mather Toronto
Client: Unilever Canada

The changing media landscape

Other outdoor media such as digital displays, interactive posters, lighting installations and projections, together with ambient and guerrilla-marketing stunts, are all part of advertising's future. Allied to this is the rise of social networking as a medium for carrying what is arguably the most effective form of advertising there is: *word of mouth*. At the forefront of this new surge of advertising approaches has been the emergence of viral advertising.

A way with words: Viral advertising

This refers to advertising that tends to use established social networks as a vehicle to raise brand awareness or achieve other strategic objectives. Viral adverts and promotional material can take a variety of forms, ranging from video clips and images to text messages. The key characteristic of a viral advert is the compulsion that the recipient feels to then send the advert on to other people within the same social network. In this way, the advertising message passes from person to person, spreading exponentially outwards, in a similar fashion to a pathological virus.

Integrated media campaigns

It is important to point out that truly integrated campaigns think beyond just the advertising. They should integrate with all other areas of brand communication, from design to public relations. As an art director, *you* are responsible for having a wider vision beyond just the single advertising media that you are working on at any one time. Look for opportunities across all advertising media and then look at how your idea can extend to other related fields of brand communication, such as pack design and sales promotion. This ability to think more holistically in terms of how your idea can encompass all areas of marketing communication is always impressive, particularly if you can demonstrate this in your book.

Making the idea go further

In terms of advertising effectiveness, using a variety of different media across a campaign can extend both the reach and the impact of the advertising message. A well-considered media plan targets the right audience with the right media, and schedules the timing and placing of that media to work synergistically to achieve the maximum effect. For example, the launch of a new brand may typically commence with a TV campaign to assure maximum exposure, and rapidly reach a large percentage of the population.

As the frequency of the TV slots is reduced, a poster campaign may be launched to promote recall of the TV commercial and prolong the initial effect. The desire and interest that TV, posters, and perhaps radio would generate could in turn drive consumers to a website or printed literature where they can find out more details about the brand. At the same time, magazine or press adverts would expand on the proposition introduced in the posters and TV or radio commercials, sometimes relaying more detail in the body copy, such as specifications, testimonials and other reasons to buy.

Below and left
Opportunities for integrated media campaigns
By focusing on the traditional rivalry between North and South Londoners, Nike created the first ever mass-team running event. This was promoted with an integrated media campaign.
Agency: Wieden+Kennedy London
Art Director: Lucy Collier
Client: Nike
Copywriter: Darren Wright
Creative Directors: Tony Davidson, Kim Papworth
Digital Agency: AKQA London
Illustrator: David Foldvari
Photographer: Til Hunter
Typographer: Richard Hooker

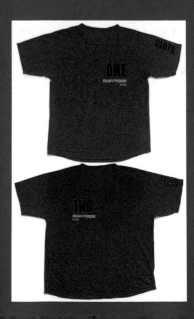

Integrated media campaigns

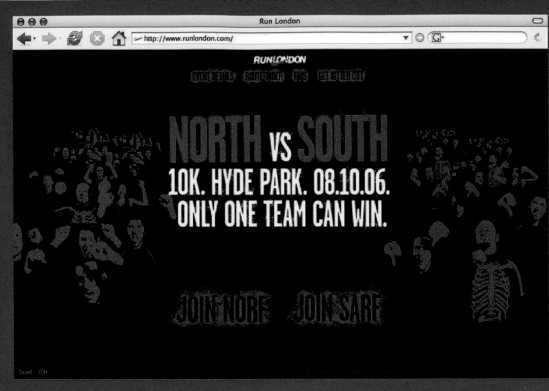

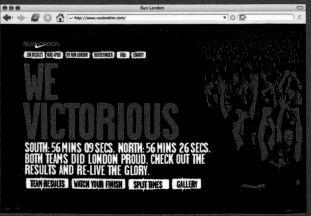

Left

Integrating the idea across different media

Nike's 'Run London' campaign included posters, press, online and retail design. The event itself attracted 17,500 runners in each team.
Agency: Wieden+Kennedy London
Art Director: Lucy Collier
Client: Nike
Copywriter: Darren Wright
Creative Directors: Tony Davidson, Kim Papworth
Digital Agency: AKQA London
Illustrator: David Foldvari
Photographer: Tif Hunter
Typographer: Richard Hooker

Give it a go

The best advertising ideas should be versatile to use across a variety of advertising media. Revisit your book and select some of your best campaign ideas. Choose a campaign where you've only generated ideas in a single medium; typically posters, press or television. Set yourself a challenge to extend your idea across at least three other advertising media. Don't simply remove the body copy from a press advert and call it a poster – you've got to work harder than that to impress! Look at the way in which you've expressed the advertising proposition and explore alternative ways of underlining it that fit the theme you've already developed – and that, most importantly, lend themselves to the medium you choose.

Ultimately, the best creative ideas are transportable across all advertising channels and can be the hub of a multimedia campaign. Student books that demonstrate integrated media thinking will always have an edge over those that exclusively contain single media concepts or one-off ideas that have little 'campaignability'.

The process of having ideas
may seem completely separate
from the task of art directing
an image. However, as you've
probably gathered by now, both
are inextricably linked. The idea
comes first, and even though
the art direction may sometimes
embody some part of the idea,
in most cases it serves to bring
the idea to life and make the
advertising message clearer
and more powerful. Having
lots of creative solutions to
help promote a brand or raise
awareness of it, is at the heart
of your role as an art director.
Everyone can have great ideas,
but when your livelihood is
dependent on being creatively
inspired on a regular basis it gets
tougher. This chapter sets out to
provide you with some insights
on how to ensure that your ideas
keep flowing!

Creative fuel

As an advertising creative, it naturally follows that you're expected to sustain a reasonably high level of creative fluency. Of course, even the most experienced creatives are prone to have a bad day, where ideas just don't seem to be forthcoming. Sometimes, you'll find that the harder you try, the more difficult it seems to have a breakthrough idea. It's at times like these that you need to draw from other resources in order to move forward and get inspired. Think of these resources as providing your 'creative fuel'. Creative fuel can come in a variety of formats and may comprise personal experiences, daily observations or existing work from a whole range of eclectic sources.

If you're hoping to produce original work, it's important that you don't simply imitate existing ideas. Instead, look at great advertising and be inspired by it.

Existing work

One way to produce great advertising is to immerse yourself in it. Be aware that a lot of the advertising we see from day to day in magazines, posters, television and other media is unlikely to be setting the creative benchmarks that you should be aiming to achieve. A useful place to find great creative advertising ideas is the award annuals produced by D&AD (Design and Art Direction) in the UK, or the Art Directors Club in the US, which showcase the best work produced from agencies across the world.

There's no better source of inspiration than to view the great work of others. Some of the best ideas can make the task look easy, but of course it's not that simple. When we see a large volume of highly creative work, it's very easy to forget that not many adverts or commercials are up to this standard.

Of course there's one big problem in viewing lots of great work. It's very easy to unwittingly copy an idea you've seen somewhere else. It may just be a case of being heavily influenced by what you've seen, but there's a risk that your own idea may become derivative of someone else's work. Sometimes it may be impossible to find a completely new idea, but there may be a way of taking an old idea and using it in a different way.

Below
Finding a source of inspiration
Viewing award-winning work can inspire you to produce great work yourself. Use periodicals and books, as well as advertising annuals, to gain familiarity with successful and popular campaigns.
Photo Nik Mahon

Creative fuel

Right:
Record your ideas and observations
You never know when that 'million-dollar' idea will surface, so be ready to capture it! Your thoughts and observations, once carefully recorded and stored, can become your creative fuel and personal archive of ideas – and possibly the first place to look when you're searching for inspiration for your next brief.
Photo: Nik Mahon

Store your thoughts and observations

One thing you can be sure of is that you're unlikely to have a breakthrough idea whilst you're staring at a blank page just waiting for it to happen. The best ideas rarely emerge on schedule and more often than not, you'll have them when you least expect them – on the train home, in the bath, at the cinema or simply when you're working on a different project. In fact, one way to help increase your chances of hitting on a novel idea when you find that you're getting stuck is to simply stop trying and go and do something else instead.

When you do have an idea, it's important to have some means of recording it quickly, such as a notebook, a camera or a small dictaphone. That way, you can be sure of capturing the idea together with any thoughts or observations you have at that moment. Your notes and records may include ideas or observations that have little or no obvious relevance to the creative task at hand or to the brief that you are working on at that time. However, if they are interesting, unusual, revealing, provocative, insightful, symbolic, metaphorical, original, or raise emotions, then get into the habit of storing them away for later.

A way with words: Cognitive fixation

'Cognitive fixation' is a condition that we have all experienced at some time or another, when we're unable to move beyond an idea to produce new ones. Some people refer to this as a 'mind-set'. Simply put, it's the technical term for 'getting stuck in a rut' and occurs when we're creatively blocked by existing ideas and routine thinking. I've refrained from using this term elsewhere in the text, but it's a great one for impressing your friends and family with!

Finding inspiration and getting ideas

Inspiration can come from a variety of sources and at any time of day or night. Some of these sources were introduced in the preceding section as providing the 'fuel' for your ideas. There are, however, many other ways of getting inspired – ranging from activities that stimulate thinking, to specific techniques for prompting ideas.

Right
The imagination of children can inspire us all
Inspiration can come from all kinds of sources. Sometimes you don't need to even leave your home to find it. This painting by Thomas and Leo Arnold, the children of Creative Director, Rosie Arnold, was one such source that helped inspire some of her work.
Painting by Thomas and Leo Arnold

Look for strange combinations or unusual contexts. Look at things from different points of view as well as close-up detail and see how that can make something more intriguing or unusual.

Visual stimulus

There are plenty of examples of advertising drawing inspiration from art. Art galleries and exhibitions can provide a fertile environment for ideas. If you're used to visiting art galleries, then try to expand your taste to view exhibitions that you wouldn't normally visit, or make a point of viewing the work of new artists or illustrators who may have fresh or unusual styles. Visual stimulus can also be found in the world about you; indoors and outdoors on the street. It often involves looking a little closer at the kind of things that we normally take for granted or may just walk past without noticing.

Finding inspiration and getting ideas

Inspiration is everywhere we look

Like many other successful advertising creatives, Rosie Arnold (Creative Director at Bartle, Bogle and Hegarty, London) draws inspiration from personal observations of the world about her, which she will often record as photographs. Everyday street furniture and signage can take on a new significance when removed from its original context. Rosie demonstrates this in each of these images, which she relates to the advertising campaign that her agency have developed for Lynx – a male deodorant (known internationally by the brand name 'Axe'). Lynx has developed a reputation for creating deodorising products with 'pulling power' (that is, the ability to stimulate sexual attractiveness) embodied by the strapline, 'The Lynx effect'. As soon as this strapline is added, the sexual connotations associated with the brand become apparent, and are reframed in a humorous fashion that fits both the brand personality and existing campaign theme. Can you work out how Rosie's photographs depict the 'pulling power' that would come to be associated with the Lynx brand?

Cuthbert's hose seemed
to have a life of its own.

THE LYNX EFFECT

Finding inspiration and getting ideas

Raiding experience

Sometimes, inspiration for an advert can
come directly from your own personal
experience, past or present. Look out
for certain patterns of human behaviour
that are common experiences, which other
people can also relate to. Here's an example.
Have you noticed how sometimes in busy,
noisy situations such as a party, we're often
too embarrassed to ask the person who's
talking to us to keep repeating themselves
when we can't hear what they're saying?
Instead, we'll try to lip-read or to pick up
on certain visual cues, such as their body
language, to guess what they are saying.
If they laugh, we laugh. If they shake their
head and frown, we shake our head and
frown. We've all done this at some time!
Now imagine what could potentially happen
if you misinterpret those visual cues and
signs. Think of the comic or embarrassing
consequences. What could you be
agreeing to, or laughing at? Now think
how this scenario could provide a storyline
for an advert or commercial – perhaps for
hearing aids, or an organisation involved in
the business of communication.

Accessing this kind of material involves
studying the way that people behave and
react in certain situations. Note down
anything that you find interesting, however
small, and keep a record of it – it's your
creative fuel!

● ● ●

**By raiding your own
experiences and
observations in this way,
it's possible to tap into
the shared experiences of
your target audience and
thereby make a connection
with them.**

Consequences

Here's a simple technique I use for prompting ideas. I call it the 'consequences' technique. The first thing to do is to identify the key benefit or feature of the product you're advertising. This shouldn't be too difficult, as it should be highlighted in the creative brief. Write this benefit in the centre of a large piece of paper. The next stage is to identify several consequences of this benefit.

For example, if the benefit of a particular brand of car is that it now comes in an open-top, convertible version, then the consequences of this benefit could be: you get more sun; you get more fresh air; you can feel the wind in your hair; you have better all-round visibility; you feel and look cool; you have extra headroom… and so on. List all of these primary consequences on the page around the central benefit.

The next stage is to now list as many consequences as you can for each of these primary consequences. Take, for example, the consequence 'you feel and look cool.' The consequences of this may, in turn, be that: you'll impress people; you'll get noticed; you'll feel good about yourself; you'll be more sexually attractive; and you'll increase your status. Once you've exhausted all the possible consequences of looking and feeling cool, move onto the next primary consequence and go through the same process.

Finally, you'll end up with a cascade of consequences resulting from the key benefit, and radiating from it in a similar fashion to a mind map. In this way, you can get to the heart of the proposition and to the real reason that your target audience may want to purchase the product (what it will really mean to them to own the product). This technique allows you to search beyond the obvious key feature of the product to the real benefit that lies behind it. In other words, you wouldn't buy the car because it has a soft-top roof, but you may buy it because it will impress your friends! You can even push this technique further to look at the consequences of those secondary consequences (for example, what would the consequences be of impressing your friends?), and with a little imagination, create a story around this.

Finding inspiration and getting ideas

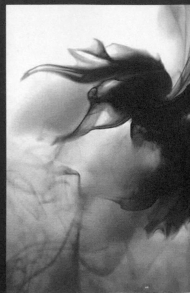

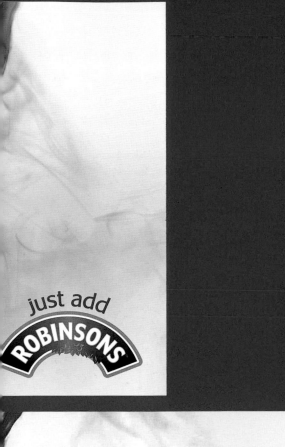

Left
Just add imagination
The images created in these adverts
for Robinsons' squash drinks are
inspired by the amorphous shapes
created when ink is poured into
water (mimicking the effect of
the squash drink being added to
water and reinforcing the slogan,
'just add Robinsons'). Clever image
manipulation enables us to visualise
a girl on a swing and a dog with a ball.
The television commercial took the
concept a stage further to have the
image dancing across the screen
to the sound of 'I Love to Boogie'
by T-Rex.
Agency: BBH London
Art Directors: Rosie Arnold,
Matt Kemsley
Client: Britvic Soft Drinks
Creative Director: Rosie Arnold
Illustrator/Retoucher: Alan Murray
Photographer: Lewis Mulatero

Emotion and empathy

One of the key skills you will need to develop is the ability to understand the hopes, desires and feelings of your audience. It's not just a case of understanding how they feel about a particular brand, but also understanding how they feel about broader issues such as current affairs or topics that may be related to the brand or have some bearing on what you say about it.

Good advertising can raise a variety of emotions with the use of skilful copywriting, scripting and direction. Try to study human emotions with a critical eye. What makes people laugh, cry, shout, rant or ask questions?

Emotion

Raising emotions can be a powerfully persuasive technique. If your advertising makes people laugh, then as long as they remember the brand message, you've taken a big step towards getting them to buy into what you have to say. Alternatively, you may need to make your audience feel sad about a particular issue. In this case, a moving piece of copy with a poignant image may achieve this. Emotions are a common language that link us all as human beings. Understanding how the combination of words and images can trigger certain emotions can enable you to make a stronger connection with your audience.

It's important to remain aware of sensitive issues and to know where to draw the line in terms of bad taste or stereotyping. However, don't shy away from being provocative and pushing the boundaries, where appropriate. As long as your advert remains honest and (of course) legal, provocation can be a useful device for getting your message heard and for eliciting a reaction from your audience.

Empathy

People are more likely to be interested in what you have to say if they first feel that you're interested in them and understand their point of view. This isn't easy if you're 21 years old, fresh out of college and are trying to write an advert for a product aimed at the over 60s market. The best thing you can do is to talk to people from within your target group and listen to what they have to say. This should also help you develop the right 'tone-of-voice' for the advert.

Ultimately, you should try to gain first-hand experience of the subject or issue that you are talking about. If your advert is aimed at raising awareness of the plight of homeless people, then actually being homeless for a few weeks would inevitably equip you with a better understanding of the problem (although – I hasten to add – I wouldn't necessarily recommend this from a personal health and safety perspective).

Give it a go

Equipped with a digital camera, a notebook and a pen, spend a morning or afternoon wandering around your local town. Your 'mission' is to notice things that you hadn't noticed before and to record your observations along the way. Look out particularly for everyday items, fixtures, building façades, architectural features, street furniture or scenes that you would normally just take for granted and walk past without a moment's thought. Look for things that make interesting or unusual images, from a different perspective or angle perhaps, or up close in detail, or when isolated from their context. One tip here is to quite literally change the way that you view things. Look upwards to the higher levels of buildings and also downwards to the ground below your feet – what can you find that you hadn't noticed before? Also, look for unusual images or street scenes that are interesting, comic, compelling or dramatic in some way, or that are likely to arouse emotions.

The objective of this exercise is to collect visual material to store as 'creative fuel' – a resource that you can refer to every time you get a new advertising brief to work on. It's not designed to trigger an idea for a project you may be working on at that time, but if that happens, then it's a bonus!

Emotion and empathy

Left:
Tapping into your audience's passion
Understanding what makes people feel passionate, and demonstrating that understanding in your advertising, is an essential ingredient in establishing a relationship with your audience. In this advert for Nike, entitled 'St Wayne', the passions generated by football and the emotions of both players and fans are captured in this evocative image of England football team striker, Wayne Rooney.
Agency: Wieden + Kennedy
Art Directors: Guy Featherstone, Chris Groom, Stuart Harkness
Client: Nike
Creative Directors: Tony Davidson, Kim Papworth
Photographer: Nick Georghiou

● ● ●

The key to really tapping into the emotions of your audience is to empathise with them. This involves having a thorough understanding of their viewpoint and demonstrating this in your advert.

JUST DO IT

How to tell whether your idea's any good

When you do get an idea for your advert or campaign, knowing whether it really is a good idea can be difficult, particularly when you've been working on it for a long time. It's sometimes easy to convince yourself that the idea must be good because it's taken so long for you to get there. When you've laboured for a considerable amount of time on a project you can be too close to it to be able to really evaluate the creative product objectively. However, there are a number of things that you can do to test the strength of your idea.

Quantity equals quality, and the more ideas that you have, the more likely you are to find a gem amongst them!

A checklist for judging your ideas

One thing you can do as an initial means of assessing your idea is to check that it meets certain criteria. Begin with the question: *'Does my solution answer the brief?'* It's very easy to get carried away with a creative idea and start drifting further from the objectives in front of you. Check also that the message is clear and simple.

Once you've done that, ask yourself: *'Is it an original idea?'* Has the idea been used in this way before? One thing to do here is to ask yourself how many other people would have had the same idea if a large group had all been given the same brief. Next ask yourself: *'Is it unexpected?'* The best adverts contain an element of surprise within them. Either something happens that you didn't expect or the idea is very unusual for its genre, grabbing attention by doing something different from the norm. In grabbing attention you can begin to engage your audience and that's the next criterion: *'Does it engage or interact with your audience?'* It can do this on an intellectual level, or an emotional level, or through entertainment or visual conundrums. Any advert that stops people in their tracks and either prompts an emotional response or gets them thinking is at the same time interacting directly with them. Assess the 'campaignability' of your idea. Does your idea have a central thought or theme that can allow it to run as a campaign, and can it work across a variety of different media? And finally, check that your highly original and creative idea is relevant – which should bring you back to the brief.

Is it on brief?	✔
Is it an original idea?	✔
Is it unexpected?	✔
Will it engage or interact with the audience?	✔
Is it addressing the right audience?	✔
Is the message or product benefit clear?	✔
Is there a big 'campaignable' idea?	✔
Is it appropriate or relevant?	✔
Do your final ideas tick all the boxes?	✔

Ask the audience

One simple but effective way to test your idea is to ask someone else what they think of it. Don't ask your best friends and relatives as they may not want to hurt your feelings. Show it to someone else, preferably a stranger from within your target audience. What do they think of it, and most importantly, do they understand the advertising message without your having to explain it? Does it have the desired effect on them?

Overnight test it

Another simple test is to hang your ideas up on your wall and forget about them until the next morning. If they still look great then, the chances are that you've cracked it! For every 'winning' idea that you have, you may have to discard hundreds, so be prepared to fill the waste bin at the end of the day!

Sometimes, the most difficult thing can be to move on from an initial 'good' idea, to a 'great' idea further on in the process. It's easy to fall in love with an early idea that can block you from having better ideas. This is why it's important to have lots of ideas first before you start judging them.

Unless you have a close friend or relative in the business, getting your first job as an art director can be a daunting task requiring patience, determination, the strength to take a few 'knocks' and the stamina and resilience to keep bouncing back in spite of them. Most of the major advertising agencies tend to hire art directors and copywriters as a team of two. Whilst there are some agencies that hire individuals, you'll have more value to the major players as a ready-made team that are already working well together. Not only that, most creatives tend to have better ideas when they have a partner to bounce those ideas off. Once you and your partner have got enough work together in your book, then it's time to start taking it around the agencies to get it seen and with any luck, get a work placement. This is the first step towards getting the job!

Putting your book together

Your book should give a clear indication of your creative potential and value to the agency. It should demonstrate your capacity for creative thinking and problem-solving in relation to a diverse range of advertising briefs. It also needs to stand alone, without the need of added commentary or explanation from you, as quite often you may be asked to leave it with the creative director or even send it to the agency by post. Be prepared to answer questions about your work and be ready to explain your thoughts; but also remember that in the real world no one is there to explain the adverts and commercials that we see and hear – we either 'get it' or we don't.

What to put in your book (and what to leave out)

The first rule about putting together your book is not to try and put everything you've ever done in there. Every piece of work should earn its place in there so be highly selective. Remember that your book is a showcase of your best ideas, so if your best is only 'average', then it may not get you very far. Having said that, you have to start somewhere and you shouldn't spend too long striving for perfection before taking your book out to a few agencies to get some feedback. Be prepared for some tough criticism, though, particularly in the early stages. It will not only help toughen you up for the task ahead, it will enable you to get a good sense of what's working and what isn't – helping you to have a better idea of what to leave in and what to take out.

It is always good to include work that you've done for major student award schemes, such as those sponsored by the D&AD and YCN (Young Creatives Network), but be aware that these are popular briefs and that there will be a lot of very similar work floating around as a result. For this reason, you should try to include a healthy balance of independent briefs that are unlikely to have been used by students on every other advertising course in the country.

When you are putting your book together, you should be aware that it is competing for attention against books from hundreds of other young creative teams that are also looking for their first break into the business. You need to find a way to make sure that your work stands out from theirs.

Steer clear from including ideas that rely on verbal puns as these are rarely appropriate and demonstrate a level of creative immaturity often associated with some of the weaker student books. Similarly, try to avoid loading your book with ideas that involve the use of sexual innuendo (unless the idea is really outstanding or incredibly funny). This tends to be quite predictable in student books, and the last thing you really want your book to be is predictable.

Structure and format

As a rule of thumb, you should normally include between six to eight campaigns in your book, and each campaign should be comprised of at least three or four ideas to demonstrate 'campaignability'. Try, however, to extend your idea to show how it would work for different advertising media. If you're including moving-image media (such as television, cinema or online), then storyboard it as clearly and simply as possible. The creatives who will be viewing your book rarely have time to read masses of script across numerous frames. If you can, keep your storyboard down to four key frames and remember that the simplest ideas are often the best.

Put your best campaigns at the front and back of your book so that they're the first and last ideas that are seen. That way, you start and finish on a high note, creating and leaving a strong – and hopefully lasting – impression on the viewer. It's also worthwhile having a digital version of your book stored on a CD that you can easily send out to agencies or leave with creatives after they've viewed the 'hard copy' with you. And finally, having your own website or blog where prospective employers can view your best work at any time will allow you to exploit every opportunity available to get your work widely seen.

Planning your campaign

Planning how you're going to
set out and land your first job in
advertising needs to be tackled
with a clear strategy in mind –
a bit like a military campaign!
Once you've put your book
together, you'll need to decide
which agencies you're going to
target and also who you'd like
to see there.

**The essence of a winning
strategy is to try and get
ahead of the competition.
If you're at college, don't
wait until the end of your
course to start getting
seen and looking for work.
Start contacting agencies
early on in your final year
in order to beat the rush
of graduates all after the
same jobs or placements.**

Have a winning strategy

The best way to draw up a list of agencies
and people to see is to look at current
advertising that you admire or aspire to,
which represents the kind of work you would
ultimately like to be doing yourself. Find out
the name of the agency and the creatives
responsible for those campaigns you admire,
and add them to your list. One way to find
out this information is by scanning the
advertising annuals, together with reading
other advertising publications, such as
Campaign magazine.

Initially, try to cast your net wide in terms
of the volume and variety of agencies that
you intend to approach with your book,
and then gradually whittle this down to a
shortlist of just a few agencies. Once they've
all seen your work and given you some
feedback, you should be able to decide
which agencies you definitely want to pursue.
Keep your options open, but you may
eventually find that you want to just target
only a few agencies, in order to focus and
channel your efforts in a more concentrated
and purposeful way.

As you begin to target a smaller group of
agencies, try to maintain regular visits to
the teams that seem to like the way that your
book's shaping up. Be focused on the goal
of getting them to offer you a placement.
If they advise you on what you need to do to
improve your book, and recommend that you
go back to see them again in a month's time,
then make the changes to your book and
return to see them two weeks later.

Above
Maintaining your book
You should constantly be
refreshing the ideas in your book
and revising them in response
to the feedback you receive from the
agencies you have visited. That way,
the work you are presenting will
get better with every visit and
will eventually open the door to
a placement.
Photo: Nik Mahon

Approaching agencies

Once you've decided which agencies you want to initially target, and who you want to see there, it's time to start picking up the phone to try and get some appointments. You'd be surprised to find that even some of the most senior creatives can remember what it was like to be looking for that first break, and are often happy to see you. In reality though, you may find that the top creative directors may not have the time to meet you, and that certain teams or individual creatives are designated to view student books and offer placements instead. Either way, it's a good start. One thing though; try to avoid seeing teams that are fresh out of college themselves. They're unlikely to be in a position to offer (or recommend) you for a placement. They're also more likely to steal your ideas!

Developing your contacts

Unless you're extraordinarily talented and extremely lucky, it's quite rare to get offered a job or a placement on your first book-viewing appointment. See every appointment as an opportunity to make contacts and pick up some good advice on how to improve your book and ultimately get that job. Never appear too defensive about your work in response to the feedback or criticism that you're given. Instead, demonstrate a willingness to return with fresh ideas and material to show that you've been able to take on board the comments that were made and, as a result, to make considerable improvements to your work.

Whenever you get a chance to get your book viewed by an agency team, use the meeting as a chance to expand your list of contacts. Ask them who else they think you should see with your book. They will have friends and acquaintances in other agencies and may even be able to tip you off on a placement that's vacant at another agency, or have inside knowledge of agencies that are currently hiring junior teams.

One last thing: when you've worked hard to develop your contacts, keep them to yourself until you've landed your first job. Remember that other students, friends or otherwise, are also competing for the same jobs!

Below
Making contact
Don't be too nervous to use the phone
and contact the people you want to
see your work. The worst they can
do is to say no; but it's more likely
they'll either agree to meet you, or will
instead provide you with an alternative
contact to approach.
Photo: Nik Mahon

What the agency is looking for

Generally speaking, when an advertising agency is seeking to hire a junior team or individuals, they're looking for people who can 'hit the ground running', who understand how to tackle a creative brief, and can generate fresh creative ideas that are strategically sound and offer a practically viable solution to the defined problem. Whilst they won't expect you to know everything from day one, they will expect you to have enough common sense, competency and creative talent to be able to get on with the job with only minimum supervision. In this sense, it is important that you adopt a professional stance: don't see yourself as part of a student team, but view yourself instead as part of a *creative* team.

Above all, you should demonstrate the capacity to see things differently, to approach problems from different angles, to challenge conventions and to apply fresh thinking to every brief you get. This alone can set you aside from all the other candidates looking for placements.

First impressions count

On a general note, remember that it's not just your creative talent that counts. Your personality, work ethic and general demeanour can express a lot about your character and personality to a prospective employer – and remember that first impressions can be hard to shift. Never be late for an appointment, try not to get too defensive about your work and make sure that all of the passion and enthusiasm that you have for advertising comes across clearly in the meeting – it may be the only chance that you'll get to demonstrate this.

Creative talent

As an art director, you will need to demonstrate the ability to generate creative ideas, and skilfully art direct them. The evidence of your creative potential naturally rests in the work that you choose to include in your book. You will need to be seen to respond to anything a viewing practitioner says about your work, in the same way that you would if you were already working at the agency and taking your ideas to show the creative director for a live project. That response will often involve taking the idea away and coming back with something better. You *can't* afford to have an artistic tantrum if you don't like what the creative director has to say or you disagree with their comments.

A word of advice here. Don't get too perplexed or confused by comments from different creatives that appear to contradict each other. All advertising creatives and their respective agencies will have different tastes, likes and dislikes upon which they will base their assessment of what's good and what's bad. Whilst one agency may like to see a more traditional type of advertising concept, another may like to see concepts that tend to break all the rules or fly in the face of normal advertising conventions. As you start to visit different agencies with your book, you should start to get an idea of which type of advertising agency you would be more suited to, then you can start to hone the work in your book towards impressing them. Remember, you can't please everyone!

Passion, persistence, energy and hunger

There'll be plenty of other students lining up for placements and jobs and, in many cases, when it comes to creative talent, there'll be little to choose between their book and yours. This is where you need to demonstrate that extra 'added value' in terms of your employability and what you would bring to the agency.

Alongside creative talent, the qualities that agencies are looking for are passion, persistence, energy and a hunger for the job. All these qualities are intertwined. They essentially indicate the kind of work ethic that will sustain you in an agency environment that often involves working long hours and the kind of commitment that requires you to really *love* what you're doing.

Persistence pays off, and if doors don't start opening straight away just keep knocking on them. It may take a couple of years to get the job you want, but if you really want it that much, then it's worth all the time and effort you invest in developing your book and getting it seen. As senior creative Billy Mawhinney once commented: 'hunger beats talent' (D&AD XChange programme, 2007).

Your book may be no better or worse than those of all the other talented teams that are looking for a placement, but if you can show that you are really hungry for it (without appearing too desperate!), then you'll have a considerable edge.

Your first placement and what happens next

Getting your first placement is a real landmark. During your placement, the emphasis shifts from improving your book to proving yourself as someone worth hiring. If you're working as a team, both you and your partner will need to pull out all the stops to demonstrate all of the qualities covered in the previous section. At the end of your placement, if the agency like what you've done and there's a vacancy going for a junior team, they may even offer you a job.

You should be applying for internships at other agencies during your first placement, ideally moving on from one placement to the next, until a job offer finally opens up for you.

Proving yourself

Once you've been shown to a desk or area where you'll be working, don't just sit around waiting for it to happen. In an ideal situation, there'll be someone to keep an eye on you, show you around, introduce you to everyone, feed you creative briefs and take a look at the work you're producing, but this isn't always the case. Agency workloads are unpredictable and you may find that your mentor doesn't always have the time to do all of this, and that after an initial welcome, you'll be left to your own ends.

Make sure that you have plenty of work to do. If you find that creative briefs *aren't* forthcoming, or that you're spending most of your time making the tea, you'll need to be more proactive in tracking down key creatives and asking for briefs. The worst thing that you can do is to become invisible over the duration of your placement. Be seen! More to the point, be seen as the placement team who kept asking for more and more briefs to work on and couldn't get enough. Remember, it's all about passion, persistence, energy and a hunger for the job!

If all goes well and the creative director likes your work, the placement may be extended. If this isn't offered, then ask them upfront whether you can stay on for a while or come back for another placement later. You've got nothing to lose by asking, and it's the kind of business where it pays to be a little bit bold (though not pushy) when you're trying to get your first job.

Above and left
Getting a foot in the door
If you're prepared to knock on enough
advertising agency doors there's a
good chance that one will eventually
open (BBH, top left; Saatchi & Saatchi,
top right; Wunderman, bottom left).
Photos: Nik Mahon

Support and resources

Once your campaign to get a job is underway, you'll need to call on all the support and resources available to make certain that everything is working in your favour, and that all of your efforts are concentrated and focused on your goal. Listed in this section are just three of the key organisations that can help you. You'll find a more comprehensive directory in the list of Useful contacts (on page 174).

The Art Director's Club

The ADC is an international, not-for-profit membership organization that provides a forum for creatives in advertising, design, interactive media and communications. Based in New York, it offers a broad range of programmes for professionals and students, and also organises year-round educational events, including workshops for high school students, scholarships, portfolio reviews and a student competition.

D&AD

D&AD is an educational charity representing global creativity in design and advertising. They sponsor an awards scheme which can fast-track students to their first job in advertising. D&AD can provide young creatives with links to agencies and offer various other opportunities for students to showcase their work, such as the workshops they run for those trying to get their careers off to a flying start. Student membership of the D&AD is available.

NABS

NABS is a benevolent organisation offering careers advice, mentoring and general support for individuals working at all levels within the marketing communications industry, from student to senior practitioner. Their resources in London include both a research library and a careers room, which is fully equipped with computers, a scanner, fax, phones and internet access. They can also provide agency contact lists and credentials, showreels, trade press and directories.

The One Club

The One Club is one of the world's foremost non-profit organizations devoted to the design and advertising industry. It provides student scholarships, portfolio reviews, annual exhibitions and competitions. The One Show College Competition gives students a chance to win a coveted One Show Pencil, whilst the Annual Student Exhibition hosts portfolio work from the best local and international graduates. Student membership is available at a nominal fee, offering the same benefits as professional membership.

Young Creatives Network (YCN)

The YCN is an organisation involved in promoting young creative talent in the design and advertising industries. Through member colleges, the YCN distributes free annuals containing live creative briefs, for which students are invited to submit ideas and solutions. Commended student work is published in the annual and exhibited at the YCN summer show. Professional development opportunities are also given by advertising agencies that sponsor YCN.

Above
The bottom line
Working on plenty of creative briefs, filling your book with ideas and getting agency feedback on those ideas is the standard route to landing your first agency job or placement.
Photo: Nik Mahon

By now you've probably gathered that the title 'art director' doesn't really provide much of a clue to the holistic and multi-faceted nature of the job role, which first and foremost involves the process of generating ideas and conceptual solutions. Whether you're working with a partner or on your own, you'll need to establish your creative strategy and have a bunch of good, 'campaignable' ideas before you can start art directing them.

Once you have the idea, art direction should be engineered to present that idea together with the advertising message, in the clearest, most impactful and memorable way possible. Words such as original, novel, compelling, unexpected, attention-grabbing, thought-provoking, and engaging also spring to mind here, as they are all qualities that you'll find in some of the best advertising today. Perhaps the most important thing to bear in mind, however, is to make sure that your attention-grabbing art direction doesn't grab all the attention away from what you have to say. Good art direction should rather help *lead* the audience *to* the advertising message or brand proposition.

Strive to grab attention in an original, compelling and unexpected way, but don't let the art direction get in the way of the brand message.

Be aware of changes that lie ahead. The advertising industry is rapidly transforming as technology advances and brands adapt or evolve to keep abreast of new demands and expectations from their customers. Whilst art direction has its roots in print-based advertising, it must now embrace new media too, which can range from online banner adverts to gargantuan digital displays or installations. Try to be one step ahead of the game, and demonstrate in your book that you have the foresight and flexibility to move with the times and experiment with ideas that can be transported across all media, new or traditional.

Finally, when you set out to get your first job, remember that perseverance pays off. It may take a while to get that first placement at an agency, but if you really love advertising, it's worth it in the end!

Here are a few terms that you've already come across in this book – some of which required further explanation, and others which are simply here as a reminder.

48- and 96-sheet posters

These are traditional poster sizes relating to the larger billboards. Both are landscape format, the 48-sheet poster measuring 120" × 240" (3048mm × 6096mm) and the 96-sheet poster 120" × 480" (3048mm × 12192mm), a massive 400 square feet.

Advertising proposition

The benefit or 'promise' that's highlighted in the advertising campaign. It's the key reason why someone should buy your brand (or buy into a particular issue or cause). It should be clear, focused, single-minded and consistent throughout the campaign.

Ambient

Advertising that tends to use or incorporate its immediate environment as part of the advertising medium itself. In many cases the advertising will remain hidden within the ambience of that environment and is only revealed once the full impact of the message has been received. It's a great way to engage an audience who don't like ads, because ambient media doesn't look or feel like traditional advertising, it takes them by surprise, and in most cases it's highly entertaining.

Art director

Normally teamed-up with a copywriter to come up with the campaign ideas, the art director is responsible for the visual look of those ideas in terms of design, layout and general impact on the page or any other advertising medium.

Book

Just another name for your portfolio. However, in advertising circles we tend to call it your 'book'.

Claymation

A stop-motion animation technique utilising a malleable material such as plasticine clay to animate characters, objects or backgrounds.

Copywriter

As the other half of the creative team, the copywriter is responsible for crafting all of the textual elements of the adverts; from headlines and straplines, to body copy and script.

Creative brief

Distilled from the client's brief and a variety of other research and data sources, this normally outlines the salient points on one or two sides of A4 paper. Most importantly it defines, in clear terms, the advertising message or proposition, the advertising objectives, the target audience, tone of voice and the advertising media to be used.

Creative team

The creative team is comprised of an art director and copywriter who, together, work on generating ideas in response to a creative brief. In some agencies this traditional partnership may be extended to include other agency specialists as part of a larger project team.

Direct advertising

Advertising that engages more directly with the key audiences by the use of sophisticated databases that enable focused targeting. Direct advertising is further distinguished by a 'call to action' such as 'click here for more details' or 'phone now for your free sample' or 'post this coupon today,' prompting a direct response from the recipient.

Flopping the image

This involves switching the orientation of everything in the image from left to right, as if it had been flipped over and viewed from its reverse side, resulting in a mirror image of the original.

Integrated campaign

A campaign where the 'big idea' is transported across all advertising media together with other marketing activities such as sales promotion and packaging.

Microsite

A supplementary site that's linked to a primary website and normally consists of one or more dedicated pages providing greater detail on a specific product, service, event, issue or similar.

Reframing

The process that occurs when an element of the communication, such as a headline or an image, changes the way we interpret that communication. Our initial ideas of 'what's going on' in the advert shifts dramatically as we look more closely. Reframing is deliberately engineered to create surprise.

Serifs

The semi-structural 'tails' that are sometimes found at the end of the typographic strokes that define the individual characters of different fonts. Most fonts are classified as either serif typefaces (with serifs) or sans serif typefaces (without serifs).

SOS syndrome

An acronym for 'same old shot' syndrome. This refers to those generic photographs we've all seen a thousand times that tend to be used over and over again for certain types of product and fail to show the product from a fresh perspective in any new, unusual or surprising ways.

Visual hierarchy

A term pertaining to the visual emphasis placed on certain elements over others. It establishes a running order in which these elements are seen or perceived when the advert is initially viewed. This enables a storyline to unfold in a certain sequence and ensures that the final 'twist' or moment of surprise in the advertising message isn't revealed too early.

Useful contacts

The Advertising Association
7th Floor North
Artillery House
11–19 Artillery Row
London SW1P 1RT
United Kingdom
Tel: +44 20 7340 1100
Fax: +44 20 7222 1504
Email: aa@adassoc.org.uk
www.adassoc.org.uk

The Art Directors Club
106 West 29th Street
New York
NY 10001
USA
Tel: +1 212 643 1440
Email: info@adcglobal.org
www.adcglobal.org

ASA (The Advertising Standards Authority)
Mid City Place
71 High Holborn
London WC1V 6QT
United Kingdom
Tel: +44 20 7492 2222
Fax: +44 20 7242 3696
Email: enquiries@asa.org.uk
www.asa.org.uk

D&AD (Design and Art Direction)
9 Graphite Square
Vauxhall Walk
London SE11 5EE
United Kingdom
Tel: +44 20 7840 1111
Fax: +44 20 7840 0840
www.dandad.org

EACA (The European Association of Communications Agencies)
152 Boulevard Brand Whitlock
B–1200 Brussels
Belgium
Tel: +32 2740 0710
Fax: +32 2740 0717
www.eaca.be

EASA (The European Advertising Standards Alliance)
152 Boulevard Brand Whitlock
B–1200 Brussels
Belgium
Tel: +32 2513 7806
Fax: +32 2513 2861
Email: library@easa-alliance.org
www.easa-alliance.org

The History of Advertising Trust Archive
HAT House
12 Raveningham Centre
Raveningham
Norwich NR14 6NU
United Kingdom
Tel: +44 1508 548623
Fax: +44 1508 548478
Email: enquiries@hatads.org.uk
www.hatads.org.uk

IAA (The International Advertising Association)
IAA World Service Center
275 Madison Avenue
Suite 2102
New York
NY 10016
USA
Tel: +1 212 557 1133
Fax: +1 212 983 0455
Email: iaa@iaaglobal.org
www.iaaglobal.org

IAB (The Internet Advertising Bureau)
14 Macklin Street
London WC2B 5NF
United Kingdom
Tel: +44 20 7050 6969
Fax: +44 20 7242 9928
Email: info@iabuk.net
www.iabuk.net

IDM (Institute of Direct Marketing)
1 Park Road
Teddington
Middlesex TW11 0AR
United Kingdom
Tel: +44 20 8977 5705
Fax: +44 20 8943 2535
Email: enquiries@theidm.com
www.theidm.com

IPA (Institute of Practitioner in Advertising)
44 Belgrave Square
London SW1X 8QS
United Kingdom
Tel: +44 (0) 20 7235 7020
Fax: +44 (0) 20 7245 9904
Email: info@ipa.co.uk
www.ipa.co.uk

NABS
47–50 Margaret Street
London W1W 8SB
United Kingdom
Tel: +44 20 7462 3150
Fax: +44 20 7462 3151
Email: nabs@nabs.org.uk
www.nabs.org.uk

The One Club
The One Club for Art and Copy
21 East 26th Street
New York
NY 10010
USA
Tel: +1 212 979 1900
Fax: +1 212 979 5006
Email: info@oneclub.org
www.oneclub.org

WFA (The World Federation of Advertisers)
120 Avenue Louise
1050 Brussels
Belgium
Tel: +32 2502 5740
Fax: +32 2502 5666
Email: info@wfanet.org
www.wfanet.org

YCN
72 Rivington Street
London EC2A 3AY
Tel: +44 20 7033 2140
Email: info@ycnonline.com
www.ycnonline.com

Recommended reading

Pete Barry
The Advertising Concept Book –
A complete guide to creative ideas,
strategies and campaigns
Thames & Hudson 2008

Rob Bowdery
Basics Advertising: Copywriting
AVA Publishing 2008

Ken Burtenshaw, Nik Mahon,
Caroline Barfoot
The Fundamentals of
Creative Advertising
AVA Publishing 2006

D&AD Annual

D&AD
The Art Direction Book –
How 28 of the world's best creatives
art direct their advertising
D&AD/Rotovision 1996

Lazar Dzamic
No-Copy Advertising
Rotovision 2001

Lisa Hickey
Design Secrets: Advertising –
50 real-life projects uncovered
Rockport 2005

Tom Himpe and Will Colin
Advertising is Dead –
Long Live Advertising!
Thames & Hudson 2008

Gavin Lucas, Michael Dorrian
Guerrilla Advertising –
Unconventional Brand Communication
Laurence King 2006

Andrea Neidle
How to Get Into Advertising
Continuum 2002 (2nd edition)

Mario Pricken
Creative Advertising –
Ideas and techniques from the world's
best campaigns
Thames & Hudson 2008

Periodicals

Campaign
Published weekly by
Haymarket Business Publications Ltd.

Creative Review
Monthly magazine
Published by Centaur: London
www.creativereview.co.uk

one. a magazine
An international quarterly magazine
for the creative advertising community
Published in the USA by
The One Club
www.oneclub.org/oc/magazine/

Online magazines

Ad Age China
http://adage.com/china/

Advertising Age
http://adage.com

Brand Republic
www.brandrepublic.com

Creativity
http://creativity-online.com

Lürzer's Archive
www.luerzersarchive.net

Acknowledgements

With thanks to everyone who made this book possible…

First and foremost, my editor Colette Meacher of AVA Publishing, who managed to keep me on track and remained a calming influence throughout this project.

Leonie Taylor, my picture researcher, whose tireless efforts and persistence enabled us to showcase some of the finest examples of creative advertising.

David Shaw, the designer, whose skill in wrestling with the pagination, my excessive word count and various other visual elements of this book deserves a special commendation.

At Wunderman, Nigel Edginton-Vigus, Karina Edginton-Vigus, Rachael Walker, Damien Knowles, Neil Williamson, Tom Redican and everyone else at the agency who gave their time and expertise to supply me with some great images for this book. Thanks also to Wunderman's client, Ford of Britain, for permission to reproduce the creative work shown.

At BBH, Creative Director Rosie Arnold for allowing me to 'borrow' her inspiring images, and Carrie Murray for helping to organise everything. Thanks also to Thomas and Leo Arnold for their fantastic painting!

At EHS Brann, Jamie Pulley and Lucy Kinmond, for the material they provided and the valuable help that they gave to my students. A special mention also for Creative Director Nigel Clifton and the support he has freely given to the Advertising course at Southampton Solent University over the past years.

The D&AD for their continued support and all of the agencies, clients, photographers, illustrators, typographers, artists, models and other individuals, too numerous to mention, who have contributed material for this book.

My thanks to the many advertising creatives who have shared their thoughts and opinions with me during conversations and interviews over the past two decades, and who have played a formative influence on my own ideas and views. To name just a few: David Abbott, Andy Dibb, Dick Dunford, John Elsom, Graham Fink, Derrick Hass, John Hegarty, Andy McGuiness, Jo Moore, Barbara Noakes, John Parkin, Simon Robinson and Andy Wakefield.

Special thanks also to all of my colleagues and students at Southampton Solent University, past and present, who have been (and remain) a motivating force for me.

Last but not least, the biggest thanks of all to my wife Tracy, and my children Kieran and Sarah, to whom I dedicate this book.